Dreams Altered

BUT NOT

Abandoned

THE TEEN MOM EXPERIENCE

by Erica Mills-Hollis

Dreams Altered

BUT NOT

Abandoned

THE TEEN MOM EXPERIENCE

by Erica Mills-Hollis

Dreams Altered
BUT NOT
Abandoned
THE TEEN MOM EXPERIENCE

Published by:
Precious Heart Publishing
6841 Virginia Parkway
Suite 103 #218
McKinney, TX 75071
Ph: (800) 387 4851
www.apreciousheart.com

Written by: Erica Mills-Hollis

Edited by: Deneen G. Matthews
Book Cover Design and Manuscript Typesetting
deeSignz Web & Graphics Studio
www.deesignz.com

ISBN: 978-0-615-41816-2

Dedication

There are a few people I would like to dedicate this book to:

First and foremost, to my beautiful, first-born son, Erique Mills – my inspiration and reason for writing this book –though it was not always easy, I still thank God that I have you and I wouldn't trade you for all the money in the world. You are truly a blessing.

Second, to my mother, Catherine Sue Thomas, where would I be without you? I was clueless about motherhood, but you showed me and taught me what I needed to know. Thank you.

Last, but not least, this book is for single and teen mommies. Although you find yourself in this situation, does not mean that you can't make it. You don't have to abandon your dreams; you just have to alter the route. Take it from me, you will make it and be stronger as a result.

Table of Contents

Foreword v

Preface vii

Introduction ix

My Teen Mom Experience xi

So You Find Out Your Pregnant.. 1

Preparing For the Arrival of Your Baby 6

Time for Baby to Arrive... 14

Money Matters... 20

Balancing School, Work, Home, and Baby 30

Continuing Your Education 35

Prevention 41

All About Birth Control... 51

The Risks: The STDs of Sex 65

Words of Wisdom: Teen Virgins.. 76

Words of Wisdom 81

Acknowledgements 103

References 105

Foreword

by Mandy Teefy

" You're just doing what you have to do until you can do what you want to do."

Words to live by; Erica Hollis openly shares her teen motherhood journey and imparts invaluable knowledge and displays of strength and endurance. It isn't just preaching. It shows what she's practiced and achieved. This is more than a do this, do that manual from a *"specialist,"* but a guided tour from a *"realist"* through her life experience, trials and tribulations.

The encouragement for teenage mothers to reach out to their community is one of the core messages of her story. I, myself, was a teen mother. I now realize how uneducated I was during my first years of motherhood. I felt alone even though I had immense support from my family. I was once told, *"You didn't only ruin your life but, you ruined your family and that child's life."*

This book can help you realize there are endless opportunities to continue a blissful and satisfying life. You just get to share them with the most important person in your life.

Preface

The number of teenage girls who get pregnant before they finish high school has quadrupled over the past few years. It's called the "babies having babies" syndrome. The number of live births to 15-19 year olds is 444,899. The birth rate for the same sample group, 15-19 year olds, is 42.5 live births per 1,000 population.

The purpose of this book is to encourage teen girls who are about to face motherhood to pursue their dreams while learning to be great mothers in spite of the odds against them and educate them to prevent reoccurring pregnancies. This book will also introduce teen girls to abstinence as the ultimate birth control choice and the alternative solution to premature pregnancy (premature acts that can lead to teen pregnancy). Each chapter includes advice and useful tips that will assist them throughout the course of their entire lives.

At the age of 16, I became a single, teen mom so I feel compelled to share my story, the challenges, and the ultimate learning experiences along the way. Who better to help you understand than someone who has experienced it themselves?

Introduction

Hello. Please let me introduce myself. I am Erica Mills-Hollis. I was your normal, average, teen girl, who fell in love at the age of 14. Of course, he was the greatest guy in the whole wide world – who I should mention – was 24 years of age at the time.

Now we all know that there was a problem with that equation. He was 24; I was 14, which equals a 10-year difference with unsuspecting moral and legal implications. A few of my family members tried to explain statutory rape laws and the legalities of that relationship, but I was so in love that I would not listen. No one could have told me it was against the law at the time. They tried, but I wasn't hearing them; I just knew that it was love and that it would last forever.

Yeah, right! Well, needless to say, I really did not have proper guidance and supervision. I did not practice abstinence; I thought it didn't apply to me. Besides, I was young and free to explore, right? How wrong was I? I knew very little to nothing about the use of contraceptives. Yes, I saw the commercials on television about birth control, but no one sat me down and explained it all in a manner that I could understand.

So, at the tender age of 15, guess what? Yes, you guessed right, I got pregnant and by *"Sweet 16,"* I had a beautiful little bundle of joy. Wow! I was still living at home with my mother, and had no earthly idea what to do next. I didn't know which way to turn. What did I possibly know about taking care of a baby? Nothing! The greatest guy in the whole wide world was around a little in the beginning. He even paid child support for about a year straight, but then, even that came to a screeching halt. I then had to rely on my mother, who was on a fixed income, to take financial responsibility, not only for me, but also for my baby. This caused major conflicts at home and brought undue hardship on my mother.

My life fell into a serious rut. I didn't have the benefit of anyone encouraging me to do more with my life, so I did what *I thought* was the best thing at that time. I dropped out of high school, and ended up getting my GED. The worse thing you can do is drop out of school. Education is a key factor to life success overall, but for a teen mother, it is imperative to remain in school. I didn't realize that until later in life. Now that I have given you that important tidbit, you have an advantage. As time went on, I secured a few decent jobs, learned a few skills, and took pretty good care of my son.

Somehow, that wasn't enough for me, and at the age of 26, I decided to finally go back to school. I wanted to prove to myself, as well as be an example to my son, that in spite of the mistakes I've made, *"a dream altered is not a dream abandoned."* If you engage faith mixed with hard work, anything in life is possible.

In 2009, at 31 years of age, I received my Associate of Arts Degree from Collin County Community College. It took me four-years to receive a two-year degree, but I was also employed full-time. I was exhausted, but I kept going no matter how difficult it became, I was determined to finish strong. Let me tell you, it was well worth it. Currently, I am pursuing my bachelor's degree. You see, I still haven't given up, and neither should you.

My Teen Mom Experience

I can still remember; like it was yesterday. It was the summer of 1994 when I heard those four life-changing words, *"Erica, you are pregnant."* I sat on the edge of the table in the cold doctor's office with a hundred emotions flowing through me.

My first thought was, *"What is my grandmother going to say?"*

After all, she is the one that instilled the faith of the Lord in me. She was the one who increased my understanding of who God really is, and all that He is able to do. I knew in my heart that I was letting her down. I was no longer going to be her little *"precious heart"* who sat on her foot rest and never left her side.

I made a grown-up decision but deep down inside I really didn't want to be grown. I was a small town East Texas girl with a heart as big as the state she lived in. I knew right from wrong, so how did I make such a huge mistake? Fear started to get the best of me and all I wanted to do was go back to being Mother Dear's *"precious heart."*

The next wave of emotions included the feeling of, *"Oh no, everything I planned to do was no longer an option."* I always made great grades, and was a good student, so I had a plethora of options. My plans were to attend Spellman University and complete a major in broadcast journalism. I had it all figured out, the plan was laid out, until I heard those four big words that now seemed to echo in my head, *"Erica, you are pregnant."*

The last emotion was a misguided emotion that I thought was real; momentarily, it was a slight feeling of bliss as my mind entertained the thought that the father of my baby would ask me to marry him once I told him the news and we would then live happily ever after.

You see, in my family, the only example of marriage and stability I witnessed was my grandparents. They remained married and together until my grandfather died in 1995. My grandmother passed away a little later in 2008. They were married for more than fifty years. There will never ever be another S.B. and Helen Ruth Mills. God broke the mold after He created those two. What a blessing!

The story is quite different, however, for both of my parents. They each had been married multiple times, and my mother is single (happily) to this day, and now my father is in another problematic marriage. I wanted desperately to break that chain. My 15-year old mind was telling me that I would be different. I thought I had the greatest guy in the world and we would prove everyone wrong. What my young naïve, 15-year old mind didn't know was that months before the baby was born, I would no longer have the greatest guy in the world.

While I missed school and was not able to enjoy the many activities of a normal 16-year old, my great guy was out there living his life to the fullest. I still remember my "Sweet 16" birthday. I was lying in bed praying that the nausea would go away; and while I was a disappointment to all the people who loved and cared for me, my great guy didn't have a care in the world.

Sometimes I sat and cried when I thought of my friends who used better judgment and totally avoided this situation. I asked myself, "Why didn't I love myself enough to prevent this from happening?" When I became an adult I finally realized that I was looking for the attention of a male who loved me undeniably; and it was not my great guy.

I know what you're thinking, "Where was your father?" My father was around sometimes, but he also had a life. His life that took up most of his time, and with his unused time, I tried to get in where I fit in.

If you'd ask me if I have any regrets, looking back, I would say the only one I have is not waiting until I was married to have sex. What I want more than anything is to be pleasing in the Lord's sight and to do everything according to His plan. I would have also loved to give my husband the gift that no one has ever had on my wedding night. How many people in this day and age can honestly say that?

As I move forward in life, I made a promise to teach my children the right way. Hopefully everyone can learn from my mistakes, and then it will not have been in vain.

one So You Find Out You Are Pregnant

The first order of business is to stay calm; do not panic. In the beginning, this will all seem very scary. Who am I kidding? The entire process is scary. You must stay strong and keep the faith; and believe that God will see you through. Yes, God. I knew of God before, but my experience as a single, teen mom, caused me to mature immediately, as well as grow up spiritually.

Now it's time to face the daunting task of telling the person(s) you're most afraid of; the person(s) you never want to disappoint – your parent(s).

It's natural to feel apprehensive about how they will react to your news. Chances are they will be very disappointed, hurt, and/or maybe even angry, but they need to know. I know it's difficult; I've been there; trust me; this is when you're really going to need them the most. If for some reason you feel you are unable to go to your parents, talk with another family member, someone in your church, or even a school counselor for sound advice and good – preferably godly direction.

Now, I am not at all advising you to keep your pregnancy from your parents, I'm only suggesting that you may feel more comfortable having someone else there with you for additional support. You must be honest with your parents. They may ask a lot of questions and share their thoughts and opinions. It may be difficult to hear, but remember, what you do effects those around you. It's probably good advice, so hear them out. Also be up front and honest and disclose the identity of the father.

I remember the day the doctor told me and my mother that I was three months pregnant. The disappointment in her eyes was so evident. I knew I had hurt her deeply. All I could think about was, *"What is my grandmother going to think? What am I going to do now?"* I had so many future plans that were

---

"...my experience as a single, teen mom, caused me to mature immediately, as well as grow up spiritually."

now put on hold because of my carelessness. I knew right from wrong, so I asked, "How could I be so stupid?"

Well, it was too late and there was nothing I could do, but learn to be a good mommy; whatever that meant. I really had no idea what I was in store for.

My mother's words rang loud in clear in my ears. She said, *"Erica, just remember this is your baby. I will be there for you, but again this is your baby."* Reality kicked in and motherhood was on its way. Next, it's time to share the news with the father of the child you are carrying. You may want to have your parents present just in case he doesn't take the news very well. If the father's parents are available, include them as well since this will be a great time for all parties involved to sit together collectively and explore all options. Let's face it, your parent(s) are going to be the ones who you will rely on for instruction, guidance and even financial support, so they have a say in the matter.

Now may be a good time to develop a relationship with God and a healthy prayer life. You will need to be in prayer requesting strength, courage, and wisdom to make it through the current and pending challenges. You have some long days and nights ahead of you, so strap in and get ready for the ride. Don't give up. Be strong. You will make it through. Be sure to surround yourself with positive influences; people who have your best interest at heart. Distance yourself from negative people, naysayers and condemners. The last thing you need is for negative energy to be transferred to you and your unborn child.

Just because you are in this situation, doesn't mean that you have to abandon your dreams. Yes, you will have to work harder, but they are still a real possibility. There are so many resources available to assist you.

Search websites that are informative, and provide a multitude of information regarding women's health, teen and single mom, support, and birth control.

Exploring Your Options

Adoption

If you feel as though you and the father are unable to successfully care for the child, you may want to consider adoption. This doesn't mean that you are a failure; it means that you are honest and responsible enough to do what is in the best interest of the child. There are so many families who want children and are unable to conceive on their own, so if adoption is an option or consideration, you know there are a host of families looking to care for a newborn baby.

Here are a few adoption websites for you to look into:

www.allforchildren.org

www.theadoptionguide.com, and

www.adoptionservices.org

According to the U.S. Department of Health and Human Services, 57,000 children were adopted in the U.S. in 2009. Adoption agencies perform extensive background checks, and have specific requirements for a family to be adoption eligible.

Some of the recorded requirements are financial stability, age criteria (must be at least 21 years of age), adequate sleeping accommodations, proper completion of the application, and concession to a thorough home inspection. Always make sure that you reach out to accredited adoption agencies to avoid any potential problems. I can't stress this enough, keep your parent(s) in the loop and ask them for their input and advice.

Mommies, remember that there can be backlash with anything that you do. Be aware that some people feel that by choosing adoption, you are taking the easy way out. That's not true. If you know that you can't properly provide for and take care of this baby, know that there is someone out there who can. No matter what, keep your head held high.

Abortion

This last option, because of my upbringing and belief, was not an alternative at all. In my attempt to provide you with as much information as possible, the reality is that most clinics or agencies, upon investigation of your options, will present abortion as an alternative to having birth. I would like to share another way to view the implication of abortion. It involves more than a procedure that eliminates the responsibility attached to the pregnancy. There are spiritual, mental and physical (health) aspects of this decision that need to be addressed. This way any decision to explore this as an option, will present all the ingredients to make an informed decision.

When you look at abortion statistics it's indeed a topic of great concern. There is controversy around whether or not a fetus is a life, the fact that it is called an "abortion" would imply that there is a process that has begun that needs to be terminated in order to cut off its existence… in this case the process is the development of a life.

An abortion decision can also have psychological effects —anywhere from immediate to later in life. The mind could begin to journey down a road of despair of what could have or should have been; leading to potential plagues of guilt ridden emotions and potential depression.

> **…the fact that it is called an "abortion" would imply that there is a process that has begun that needs to be terminated in order to cut off its existence…**

From a physical perspective, there are major health risks associated with abortion procedures. According to Burkman's **"Morbidity Risk Among Young Adolescents Undergoing Elective Abortion,"** endometritis is a post-abortion risk for all women, but teenagers are 2.5 times more likely than women 20-29 to acquire this post-abortion condition. Endometritis is an inflammation or irritation of the uterine lining.

Other risks also include the risk of death, infection, excessive bleeding, pregnancy complications later in life, possible infertility, as well as other spiritual and psychological implications.

Ladies, you must factor in the spiritual, mental and physical health aspects before making these decisions. You don't want to make a NOW gratifying decision that will have a tremendous affect in the years to come.

Yes, it's a lot to think about, but you must weigh all the options along with all the consequences and make informed choices; ones that you will be forced to live with. If everyone comes together and comprises a list of pros and cons, based on all of your options, I'm sure a decision will be made that is suitable and in the best interest of the parents and the life of the baby.

Prenatal Care

Developing a course of action in this area should be treated with urgency, because whether the choice is to keep the baby or seek out adoptive parents, you will need prenatal care.

Prenatal care should begin within the first few weeks after you confirm your pregnancy. If there are any health problems or concerns for you or the baby, early detection by your physician will allow for early treatment; as opposed to them finding out later on in your pregnancy and not being able to treat you. Be intentional about maintaining good healthy habits throughout your pregnancy and don't take unnecessary chances regarding you and your baby's health.

Preparing for the Arrival of Your Baby

Mommies it's time to get down to the nitty gritty. By now, you have told your parents, the father of your child along with his parents and have decided to keep your baby; so what's next?

Healthy Home . Healthy Mom . Healthy Baby

First mommies, let's survey the home front. Healthy mom, healthy baby also requires healthy living conditions. If you are in an unstable home where there is abuse or neglect, there is a program that can provide you with housing assistance.

Second Chance Homes

This HUD-driven program is called Second Chance Homes. A direct quote from their website describes the program in the following manner:

"Second Chance Homes are adult-supervised, supportive group homes or apartment clusters for teen mothers and their children who cannot live at home. Nationwide, at least 6 states have made a statewide commitment to Second Chance Home programs: Massachusetts, Nevada, New Mexico, Rhode Island, Texas and Georgia. In statewide networks, community-based organizations operate the homes under contract to the states and deliver the services. States share in the cost of the program; refer teens to homes, and set standards and guidelines for services to teen families. In addition, there are many local Second Chance Home programs operating in an estimated 25 additional states."

Aside from housing assistance, this program offers many life assistance tools in cases where you may not have parental support. Remember, you are not alone and there is an onslaught of aided programs available. HUD's Second Chance Homes provides an adult-supervised, supportive living arrangement, a mandatory requirement to finish high school or obtain a GED, as well as access to other human and support services such as child care, health care, transportation, counseling, parenting and life skills classes, education, job training, and employment services.

More information is available via their website at www.hud.gov.

Finding a Physician

Now it's time to find a good physician. As I stated earlier, the sooner you find a doctor, the better. You don't want to run the risk of having an unhealthy baby or doing harm to your own body. If you already have an OB-GYN (Obstetrics and Gynecology), then you are all set. If you do not have an OB-GYN, but have a general practice physician, you are still in good shape. Your general practitioner can provide you with a referral and make a recommendation for an OB-GYN who can meet all of your needs.

Location | Transportation

One of the most important factors when looking for a doctor is office location. Finding a doctor that is closer to home is ideal and will assist you with making all of your scheduled visits. If your situation is anything like mine, you may need to rely on family members and friends for rides back and forth to your appointments, unless you are fortunate enough to have a car of your own. If your doctor's office is close by, people will be more willing to provide transportation. With today's gas prices, the closer you are the better.

Alternatively, check local mass transit for possible bus or train routes to and from the doctor's office. If all else fails and you can't get a ride to your appointments, public transportation will always come through for you. There should be a transit website with information on bus and/or train routes, schedules and fare information. Hey, it may not be your preferred mode of transportation, but it will get you where you need to go. Just look on the bright side; this is only temporary. You're going to be very successful and one day, you'll be able to drive the vehicle of your choice. You're just doing what you have to do until you can do what you want to do. These are words to live by.

How Can I Afford a Physician?

Insurance

So back to the subject matter; we've discussed location. The next major factor is cost. Indeed it is expensive to have a baby, so there is a lot to consider. If you just happen to be on your parents insurance, most of your expenses should be covered depending on coverage and deductibles. You might also inquire as to whether your baby's father can help out with any of these expenses. If you are in a position where you don't have insurance or financial support, you can apply for Medicaid.

Medicaid

Medicaid is a state-run program that provides medical insurance for low-income individuals. Each state has different eligibility requirements and different application procedures. Contact your local state Department of Social or Human Services and find your local Medicaid office. You will have to appear in person to complete the application. Ask office personnel for assistance if you have any questions about how to complete the form; do not guess at anything. You will need the following documents in order to complete the application process: birth certificate, driver's license, pay stub (that is if you are working), social security card, and proof of residence.

Medicaid covers all costs associated with your pregnancy, labor and delivery. It also covers any complications during pregnancy or up to 60 days after your baby's birth. If you are receiving Medicaid benefits when your child is born, both you and your child are covered. So when choosing a physician, make sure they accept Medicaid as a form of payment. For more Medicaid information you can visit their website: *www.cms.hhs.gov/home/medicaid.asp.*

> **"You're just doing what you have to do until you can do what you want to do... words to live by."**

Your First Appointment

Once you have secured a doctor and have ample coverage, schedule an appointment immediately. During your first visit, you can expect to have a full physical, to include: a pelvic exam, blood work, and urine samples. The pelvic exam is taken to test for cervical cancer or other STD's (sexually transmitted diseases). Blood is drawn to calculate your blood count and aid in the detection of STD's. Urine samples test sugar and protein levels. Keep in mind, all of these tests are routine. If you have any questions about your results, speak to your health care provider.

More than likely, before you leave the doctor's office, you will have your baby's due date and a supply of prenatal vitamins. Please take the vitamins;

they are essential to the proper growth and development of your baby. If the vitamins make you sick to your stomach, just ask the doctor for another brand, but don't just stop taking them.

In the beginning, you will visit your doctor every four weeks for the first 28 weeks; then every two weeks until you reach the 36 week mark and finally every week until your baby arrives. Yes, that's a lot of appointments, but well worth it.

During your pregnancy you may experience a few symptoms. Now everyone's body is different, so this may or may not even apply to you. You may experience, nausea, vomiting, leg cramps, heartburn, backache, fatigue, and swollen ankles. If you happen to experience severe bleeding and painful stomach cramps you need to contact your doctor immediately. On the other hand, you could be the mommy that has no harsh symptoms and full of energy. You just never know.

What I do know is that you need to maintain a healthy diet and lifestyle. You're not eating for just you anymore; you're also eating for your unborn child. You're going to get some crazy cravings, but try to fight eating poorly. Mommies, I know you can do it. Eat plenty of fruits, vegetables, grains, dairy, beans, and cooked meat. You should avoid seafood that contains high levels of mercury such as shark, swordfish, king mackerel, or tile fish – to name a few. They can cause serious damage to the baby's brain development. During and outside of your pregnancy, you want to avoid smoking, drinking and drug use. These simple guidelines will help promote a healthy and complication-free pregnancy.

The Golden Rule: Stay in School

Ladies, if you're in the middle of a school year, please continue to attend. Education is very detrimental to your future. I know there will be mornings when you feel like you just can't make it, but you absolutely must for the sake of your baby. In March 2010, President Obama distributed the *"Steps to Reduce Dropout Rate and Prepare Students for College and Careers"* press release.

It states that, *"Every school day, about 7,000 students decide to drop out of school – a total of 1.2 million students each year – and only about 70% of entering high school freshman graduate every year. Without a high school diploma, young people* *are less likely to succeed in the workforce. Each year, our nation loses $319 billion in potential earnings associated with the dropout crisis."*

These figures are way too high and I want you to be a part of the 70% success graduate rate and help the numbers increase toward 100%. I probably sound like a hypocrite to you, because I shared in the introduction that I dropped out and got my GED. Well, my desire is for you to be and do better than me. I took what appeared to be the easy way out, and regret that decision to this day. There is nothing like having your high school diploma hanging on the wall. I totally missed out on that formality. So, let's earn those diplomas, mommies.

Schooling Options and Programs

Homebound

In some schools, there is a program call Homebound. Homebound is designed for students who normally and regularly attend school, but are confined to their home or hospital because of an illness or accident for a period of ten (10) or more consecutive days. Inquire with your school counselor to see if your facility offers this program. Not all guidelines are the same; they vary from school to school. It could be that your parent(s) will have to go to the school every few weeks to retrieve all your home work assignments and tests or maybe a certified instructor will be assigned to come to your home and establish your lesson plans.

If there is no such program in place at your school, try to get as far as you can and complete all of your assignments while you are in attendance, so that after you have the baby you won't be too far behind. It's better to play catch up, than to start all over again.

Alternative School

If your school isn't willing to work with you in this situation, you might try and find an alternative school. I know what you're thinking, *"I don't want to go to school with a bunch of bad kids."*

Well, let me inform you, alternative schools are not just for kids with behavior problems. Alternative schools are institutions that provide alternative education arrangements. It is an educational establishment with a special curriculum of non-traditional teaching methods; offering a more flexible program of study. This may actually be a suitable alternative for you. This could mean; smaller classroom settings, less hours a day, and even working assignments at your own pace. Just don't give up; no matter what it takes. Check and see if your city has an alternative school specifically for teen parents. Most of these schools even have on-site day care centers, so that after you have your baby, you can come back to school without worrying about day care.

An online article on livestrong.com, talks about alternative schools, and states, *"Due to the responsibilities that come with being a parent, many teen mothers find it difficult, if not impossible, to finish their high school educations. A 2008 "Wall Street Journal" report notes that high school graduates earn roughly $300,000 more over their lifetimes than those who dropped out of school early. Thus, finishing high school can give a teen mother a considerable financial advantage. Many school districts offer alternative school programs for pregnant teens and teen mothers. These alternative programs allow teen mothers to earn their high school diplomas while also learning valuable parenting skills. While each program varies, some allow teens to bring their children with them to class while others provide shorter school days to allow teen mothers more time with their children."*

Mommies, you have options. A lot of these programs did not exist back in the day, so please take advantage of them and turn your challenge into a triumph.

Supplies

Now that you know your schooling options, let's talk about all the supplies you need for your newborn. You're going to need to have most of your supplies in your possession before your baby arrives. Can you say baby shower time? Yeaaaaah – the fun stuff!!! Babies require a lot, but have no fear; I'm going to help you with everything you need.

First things first, you need furniture. I know, money is really tight, so we're going to improvise a little. Instead of a crib, try to find an inexpensive bassinet. If your budget won't accommodate a bassinet, try garage sales or even a second-hand store. Hey, do not be ashamed of the hand me downs. Remember, we do what we have to do, until we can do what we want to do. Things like the dresser and changing table can wait until money is not so funny. Just make room in your dresser drawers and that will work just fine.

Now, you need a car seat and you need one with a head cushion insert installed. You will not be able to take your baby home from the hospital without it. Make sure you have it installed before you go into labor. It's a state requirement and the safest way to transport your baby in any automobile. Infants must have rear-facing car seats until they are – at a minimum – 1 year old and at least 20 pounds. The rear forward facing seats are for toddlers, ages 1 to 4 and/or from 20 to 40 pounds. Booster seats are for toddlers, ages 4 to 8 and under 4'9" in height. Always strap your child into the car seat and if you're not sure how to install the seat, please ask for help.

You will need formula (which the doctor will assign after delivery), if you choose not to breast feed. You will also need a few 4 to 6 oz. bottles, nipples for the bottles, pacifiers, and a bottle brush for cleaning purposes. If you decide to breast feed, you need a breast pump machine, breast pads, nipple cream, and nursing bras.

Your equipment needs will be a diaper bag, stroller, a diaper pail (if you can afford one), if not a plastic baggie will work just fine, and an infant bathtub.

Your linen needs are bassinet sheets, burping cloths, receiving blankets, washcloths, and bath towels. If you purchased a crib instead of a bassinet you need crib sheets, crib blankets, quilted crib pads, and waterproof mattress pads.

Clothing depends on the weather, but things you will need in spite of the season are bibs, no-scratch mittens, booties or socks, snap onesies, snap undershirts, t-shirts, and hats. Shoes are really optional at this point because your baby will not come out walking. More than likely he or she will sleep a lot in the beginning, so comfortable clothes are always great. Optionally, if you are a fashion bug and want your baby to be sporty, go ahead and get different shirts, pants, shorts, and things of that nature. Just keep in mind, you're on a budget.

Sanitary and hygienic items include but are not limited to, plenty of diapers, wipes, gentle baby soap, gentle baby shampoo, diaper-rash ointment, brush and comb set, baby nail scissors, cotton swabs, gentle laundry detergent, vaseline, gas drops, first-aid kit, thermometer, and a nasal aspirator. If you are fortunate to have a baby shower, stress the need for diapers. They are quite costly, but the most needed item.

When your baby gets a little older, you will need things like sippy cups, teething rings, toys, feeding spoons and bowls, a high chair, store cart covers, doorknob covers, outlet covers (for electrical sockets), and bouncer seats.

Keep Your Bags Packed

Before your delivery due date, be sure to have a bag packed for you and your baby. In mommy's bag, be sure to include the insurance or Medicaid card(s), comb and brush, toothbrush, toothpaste, slippers, cell phone (if you have one), cell phone charger, gowns, socks, a going home outfit, lotion, deodorant, soap, sanitary napkins (you will have a period that will last a couple of weeks), and breast feeding equipment (if that is your feeding choice). In the case of a cesarean birth (c-section), your stay could be anywhere from 3 to five days. With natural child birth, free from complications, you will probably only stay in the hospital for a couple of days. Just be certain to pack enough essential items either way.

Baby's bag will contain a going home outfit, diapers, blankets, bibs, a few bottles, mittens, and socks. The hospital will most likely give you a few diapers to take home, but to be on the safe side, take some with you.

Be Appreciative

Don't forget to send thank you cards or thank you notes, if the cards are too expensive, to everyone. You want to express and display your gratitude for everything they have done for you. Gratitude goes a long way. When people are appreciated, they are generally willing to extend themselves and pitch in when needed. My mother always told me, *"You never want to burn bridges. You never know when you may have to cross it again."* Boy is that wisdom.

three

Time for Baby to Arrive

Labor & Birth

Now it's time for your baby's world debut appearance. You may have a scheduled cesarean procedure or contractions kick in and turn your whole world upside down. Again, everyone is different, and you could very well be the one who experiences no pain at all. Unfortunately, I had the pain. It's important not to panic. If your parent(s) are there, let them know what's going on.

You can either call the doctor so they can meet you at the hospital or you can just go directly to the hospital. A call in to the doctor first is recommended, because this could be a false labor. False labor is when you experience pain, but it's not time to deliver the baby. This is quite common, so don't worry. If you are in labor, remember to grab the bags previously packed for you and your baby.

I can remember like it was yesterday. I felt a sharp pain in my side at 3:00 am. I jumped out of bed and ran into mother's room. I swung open her door and said, "Oh my God, I just felt the worst pain in my life." My mother knew instantly that I was going into labor. She grabbed my bags, told me to change my clothes and we were on our way.

We got to the hospital about 30 minutes after my first pain and that's when the torture began. Eleven hours later I was still pregnant and in pain. A woman usually gives birth when she dilates about ten centimeters. After eleven hours, I had only reached one centimeter. How horrible is that? I was tired, frustrated and ready to give birth.

About an hour later, my doctor realized that my birth canal was too small to give birth naturally, so he suggested a cesarean. I was so relieved, because I just knew the pain was almost over. Thirty minutes later the anesthesiologist arrived and administered an epidural in my spine and the pain went away. I was then wheeled to the delivery room where the nurses strapped my hands down and placed a blue sheet in front of me so that I couldn't see what they were doing. I felt the movement and pressure of the doctor moving around in my stomach, but I couldn't feel the pain.

About ten minutes later I heard the sweetest little cry I ever heard in my life. One of the nurses brought my baby around the sheet and when I saw him, my heart melted. This sweet, little, precious baby was worth all the pain I encountered. At that moment I made up my mind that I would be the best mommy I could be. I would not let little Erique down.

After delivery, you will be in the care of the doctors and nurses. This is a really good time to ask any and all questions you may have. These competent medical professionals will adequately address your concerns. If you feel you may not be feeding, changing, or burping the baby correctly, they will assist you and demonstrate how to do it properly.

It's Official! You're a Mommy

Here's where reality sets in. You are officially a new mommy. I can't tell you not to be afraid, because it is a very scary scenario. You are now totally responsible for the life of another human being. Don't worry; your motherly instincts will kick in full throttle. As much as possible, try and keep your baby in the hospital room with you. Right after giving birth, the medical staff will let you spend a few minutes with your newborn, so that you are the first person to bond with him/her. The first moments of a baby's life need to be spent with you, so that you both can form that initial bond. They are then taken to the nursery for a good bath and a pediatric physician is assigned to your baby. They will administer several tests and shots consisting of a vitamin K injection to help the blood clot, a hepatitis vaccine, a newborn screening blood test, and a blood sugar level check.

Try and get as much rest as possible. Having a baby takes a major toll on your body. You may experience fatigue, severe bleeding with some clot drainage, and even some depression. Postpartum depression can occur in various degrees and usually sets in within days of delivery and/or even up to a year later. Some symptoms are fear of harming the baby, severe panic, or feeling out of control. If you experience any of these feelings, please alert someone immediately so that you can get the proper help needed.

If you have a cesarean procedure, things may be a little different. For instance, your body can remain numb for a few hours after the procedure, so you won't be able to move around right away. As a safety precaution, someone will need to be present while the baby is in the room.

Your incision will be sealed with staples or stitches, which also makes movement uncomfortable. They are usually removed before you leave the hospital unless you have dissolvable stitches that dissolve on their own. There is a little more pain associated with the cesarean, than with natural child birth. Make sure you alert the medical staff about your pain, so they can give you proper medication to help ease the pain. Enjoy this time in the hospital, because help is only a push button away.

Headed Home; Get Acclimated

Now that it is time to bring your newborn home, ask any last minute questions of the medical staff before you ride out the door in your wheelchair. Before you leave the hospital, your appointed pediatric physician will inform you of when to schedule a follow up appointment for your baby. If for some reason you are not satisfied with the appointed pediatric physician, you can then select another you feel more comfortable with. You will also need to schedule a follow-up appointment with your OB-GYN, generally within the first couple of weeks after discharge.

When you finally get home, you're going to have to take it easy. When your baby naps, learn to nap then also. If you had a cesarean delivery, ask for help with house work, laundry and things that require lifting anything that weighs more than your baby, to avoid injury that may reopen or cause excessive bleeding to your incision.

If you are using formula for feeding, make up a few bottles ahead of time so your baby doesn't get agitated waiting for one to be made. Throughout the course of the day, whenever your newborn is awake, try not to hold them every minute to avoid creating a habit. Or else you will not be able to get anything done, because the baby will want to be held all the time. Try things like a swing or a bouncer. These items will keep your newborn entertained, while you're doing chores or homework.

"The only *"sure"* and *"safe"* method of birth control and the only 100% guaranteed way to prevent pregnancy is abstinence."

Consider taking a multivitamin for energy. Some good ones are Centrum, One-a-day, and Nature Made. If you are unsure which brand to take, ask your doctor at your first follow-up, post-delivery appointment.

I must really stress the importance of proper rest and vitamins. After I was at home for the first couple weeks, it was so hard to keep up. I became frustrated because of lack of sleep and a limited amount of me time for that matter. I remember sitting on the edge of my bed holding my baby at 2:00am crying, because I was so tried. I even asked myself if I had done the right thing keeping my baby. It can happen. It didn't get better until I put a plan in motion, became proactive and started taking an energy supplement. Taking vitamins allowed me to stay a step ahead of my schedule and I was finally able to get past that moment. It took a little time to get there, but I did.

Post-Deliver Doctor Visits

Make sure you continue to attend all of your checkups; it takes a healthy parent to take care of a baby. Your first post-delivery appointment is usually scheduled four to six weeks after giving birth. Your doctor will perform a complete exam to ensure that you are healing properly. This will also be a good time to discuss any problems or concerns, so be sure to ask questions, if you have them. Your doctor will check your weight, blood pressure, and perform an internal exam to make sure there are no bruises, scratches, or tears to your cervix and observe that your vagina is healing properly, if you had a natural birth. He or she will examine your breasts and abdomen to make sure your uterus is returning to its normal size and that there are no lumps formed in your breasts.

Your doctor will probably discuss sex, present you with different birth control options, and educate you on their use and side effects. Even the most effective birth control method(s) used and taken correctly, cannot guarantee 100% prevention. Even the smallest percentage of chance is still a chance for an additional pregnancy.

Hello, now focus; SEX SHOULD BE THE LAST THING ON YOUR MIND. You have more important matters at hand, remember?

The only *"sure"* and *"safe"* method of birth control and the only 100% guaranteed way to prevent pregnancy is abstinence. The only thing harder than raising one child when you're a teen; is raising two if you are not abstaining. Mommies, I know you really don't want to hear that, but it's the truth.

Abstinence is also the only surety of not contracting any of a host of diseases you can now choose from. Contraceptives, the pill or a shot cannot protect you from contracting deadly viruses. Is it really worth it? Yeah, I know, we've all heard it; use a condom for additional protection. Well, condoms break, then what?

Well-baby Checkups

Also, be sure your baby makes all of his/her well-baby checkups. These visits are usually scheduled at 1 month, 2 months, 4 months, 6 months, 9 months, 12 months, 15 months, 18 months, and 24 months. Different provider schedules and routines may vary, of course. Be sure to ask your baby's health care provider about their particular schedule for well-baby visits.

During these visits, you can expect immunization, growth charting, general development, blood test, physical examination and nutrition and development advice. Be prepared to answer questions about your baby's eating habits and developmental skills. When it comes to immunization, it's never fun for you or the baby. I mean, who really wants to see their precious bundle of joy get stuck with a big old needle? None of us do, but it is necessary. Before you left the hospital, your nurse may have provided you with a shot record with the shot(s) your baby already received; along with the shots needed in the future. If not, I have included an immunization schedule from ages birth to 6 years old and an immunization record tracker created by Centers for Disease Control and Prevention. Both of these items can be found at *www.cdc.gov.*

When it's time for your baby to have their immunization, remember to take both the scheduler and the tracker with you. Once the immunization has been completed give the tracker to the physician so that he/she can input the dates onto your tracker. This will be very useful when you're little one starts day care or school, because shot records are required. This will eliminate you having to make additional trips to the doctor just to update your tracker.

Recommended Immunization Schedule

Recommended Immunization Schedule for Persons Aged 0 Through 6 Years—United States • 2011

For those who fall behind or start late, see the catch-up schedule

Vaccine ▼ Age ►	Birth	1 month	2 months	4 months	6 months	12 months	15 months	18 months	19–23 years	2–3 years	4–6 years	
Hepatitis B[1]	HepB	HepB				HepB						Range of recommended ages for all children
Rotavirus[2]			RV	RV	RV[2]							
Diphtheria, Tetanus, Pertussis[3]			DTaP	DTaP	DTaP	see footnote[3]	DTaP				DTaP	
Haemophilus influenzae type b[4]			Hib	Hib	Hib[4]	Hib						
Pneumococcal[5]			PCV	PCV	PCV	PCV				PPSV		
Inactivated Poliovirus[6]			IPV	IPV		IPV					IPV	Range of recommended ages for certain high-risk groups
Influenza[7]						Influenza (Yearly)						
Measles, Mumps, Rubella[8]						MMR		see footnote[8]			MMR	
Varicella[9]						Varicella		see footnote[9]			Varicella	
Hepatitis A[10]						HepA (2 doses)				HepA Series		
Meningococcal[11]											MCV4	

This schedule includes recommendations in effect as of December 21, 2010. Any dose not administered at the recommended age should be administered at a subsequent visit, when indicated and feasible. The use of a combination vaccine generally is preferred over separate injections of its equivalent component vaccines. Considerations should include provider assessment, patient preference, and the potential for adverse events. Providers should consult the relevant Advisory Committee on Immunization Practices statement for detailed recommendations: **http://www.cdc.gov/vaccines/pubs/acip-list.htm.** Clinically significant adverse events that follow immunization should be reported to the Vaccine Adverse Event Reporting System (VAERS) at **http://www.vaers.hhs.gov** or by telephone, **800-822-7967.**

1. **Hepatitis B vaccine (HepB).** (Minimum age: birth)
   At birth:
   - Administer monovalent HepB to all newborns before hospital discharge.
   - If mother is hepatitis B surface antigen (HBsAg)-positive, administer HepB and 0.5 mL of hepatitis B immune globulin (HBIG) within 12 hours of birth.
   - If mother's HBsAg status is unknown, administer HepB within 12 hours of birth. Determine mother's HBsAg status as soon as possible and, if HBsAg-positive, administer HBIG (no later than age 1 week).
   Doses following the birth dose:
   - The second dose should be administered at age 1 or 2 months. Monovalent HepB should be used for doses administered before age 6 weeks.
   - Infants born to HBsAg-positive mothers should be tested for HBsAg and antibody to HBsAg 1 to 2 months after completion of at least 3 doses of the HepB series, at age 9 through 18 months (generally at the next well-child visit).
   - Administration of 4 doses of HepB to infants is permissible when a combination vaccine containing HepB is administered after the birth dose.
   - Infants who did not receive a birth dose should receive 3 doses of HepB on a schedule of 0, 1, and 6 months.
   - The final (3rd or 4th) dose in the HepB series should be administered no earlier than age 24 weeks.

2. **Rotavirus vaccine (RV).** (Minimum age: 6 weeks)
   - Administer the first dose at age 6 through 14 weeks (maximum age: 14 weeks 6 days). Vaccination should not be initiated for infants aged 15 weeks 0 days or older.
   - The maximum age for the final doses in the series is 8 months 0 days
   - If Rotarix is administered at ages 2 and 4 months, a dose at 6 months is not indicated.

3. **Diphtheria and tetanus toxoids and acellular pertussis vaccine (DTaP).** (Minimum age: 6 weeks)
   - The fourth dose may be administered as early as age 12 months, provided at least 6 months have elapsed since the third dose.

4. **Haemophilus influenzae type b conjugate vaccine (Hib).** (Minimum age: 6 weeks)
   - If PRP-OMP (PedvaxHIB or Comvax [HepB-Hib]) is administered at ages 2 and 4 months, a dose at age 6 months is not indicated.
   - Hiberix should not be used for doses at ages 2, 4, or 6 months for the primary series but can be used as the final dose in children aged 12 months through 4 years.

5. **Pneumococcal vaccine.** (Minimum age: 6 weeks for pneumococcal conjugate vaccine [PCV]; 2 years for pneumococcal polysaccharide vaccine [PPSV])
   - PCV is recommended for all children aged younger than 5 years. Administer 1 dose of PCV to all healthy children aged 24 through 59 months who are not completely vaccinated for their age.
   - A PCV series begun with 7-valent PCV (PCV7) should be completed with 13-valent PCV (PCV13).
   - A single supplemental dose of PCV13 is recommended for all children aged 14 through 59 months who have received an age-appropriate series of PCV7.
   - A single supplemental dose of PCV13 is recommended for all children aged 60 through 71 months with underlying medical conditions who have received an age-appropriate series of PCV7.

- The supplemental dose of PCV13 should be administered at least 8 weeks after the previous dose of PCV7. See MMWR 2010:59(No. RR-11).
- Administer PPSV at least 8 weeks after last dose of PCV to children aged 2 years or older with certain underlying medical conditions, including a cochlear implant.

6. **Inactivated poliovirus vaccine (IPV).** (Minimum age: 6 weeks)
   - If 4 or more doses are administered prior to age 4 years an additional dose should be administered at age 4 through 6 years.
   - The final dose in the series should be administered on or after the fourth birthday and at least 6 months following the previous dose.

7. **Influenza vaccine (seasonal).** (Minimum age: 6 months for trivalent inactivated influenza vaccine [TIV]; 2 years for live, attenuated influenza vaccine [LAIV])
   - For healthy children aged 2 years and older (i.e., those who do not have underlying medical conditions that predispose them to influenza complications), either LAIV or TIV may be used, except LAIV should not be given to children aged 2 through 4 years who have had wheezing in the past 12 months.
   - Administer 2 doses (separated by at least 4 weeks) to children aged 6 months through 8 years who are receiving seasonal influenza vaccine for the first time or who were vaccinated for the first time during the previous influenza season but only received 1 dose.
   - Children aged 6 months through 8 years who received no doses of monovalent 2009 H1N1 vaccine should receive 2 doses of 2010–2011 seasonal influenza vaccine. See MMWR 2010;59(No. RR-8):33–34.

8. **Measles, mumps, and rubella vaccine (MMR).** (Minimum age: 12 months)
   - The second dose may be administered before age 4 years, provided at least 4 weeks have elapsed since the first dose.

9. **Varicella vaccine.** (Minimum age: 12 months)
   - The second dose may be administered before age 4 years, provided at least 3 months have elapsed since the first dose.
   - For children aged 12 months through 12 years the recommended minimum interval between doses is 3 months. However, if the second dose was administered at least 4 weeks after the first dose, it can be accepted as valid.

10. **Hepatitis A vaccine (HepA).** (Minimum age: 12 months)
    - Administer 2 doses at least 6 months apart.
    - HepA is recommended for children aged older than 23 months who live in areas where vaccination programs target older children, who are at increased risk for infection, or for whom immunity against hepatitis A is desired.

11. **Meningococcal conjugate vaccine, quadrivalent (MCV4).** (Minimum age: 2 years)
    - Administer 2 doses of MCV4 at least 8 weeks apart to children aged 2 through 10 years with persistent complement component deficiency and anatomic or functional asplenia, and 1 dose every 5 years thereafter.
    - Persons with human immunodeficiency virus (HIV) infection who are vaccinated with MCV4 should receive 2 doses at least 8 weeks apart.
    - Administer 1 dose of MCV4 to children aged 2 through 10 years who travel to countries with highly endemic or epidemic disease and during outbreaks caused by a vaccine serogroup.
    - Administer MCV4 to children at continued risk for meningococcal disease who were previously vaccinated with MCV4 or meningococcal polysaccharide vaccine after 3 years (if the first dose was administered at age 2 through 6 years).

The Recommended Immunization Schedules for Persons Aged 0 Through 18 Years are approved by the Advisory Committee on Immunization Practices (**http://www.cdc.gov/vaccines/recs/acip**), the American Academy of Pediatrics (**http://www.aap.org**), and the American Academy of Family Physicians (**http://www.aafp.org**).
Department of Health and Human Services • Centers for Disease Control and Prevention

four

Money Matters

Okay, let's get down to money matters. I'm not sure of your financial situation, but now you may either have to find work and pay bills, apply for government assistance, or both. So, let's get started.

Government Funded Assistance

If you need to apply for government assistance, remember this is a temporary source of support; not a career move. You should desire better for yourself and your child. Don't get me wrong, when you need help, don't be too proud to get help, but always aspire for more.

Health Coverage

Earlier I discussed Medicaid for health coverage benefits. If you are still unable to afford health care insurance, consult your health and human service office for insurance extensions and future care options.

Food Stamps

If you need assistance with food, contact your local social security office for information regarding food stamp eligibility. The food stamp program helps low-income families buy food for their entire household. Generally, the application must be accompanied with the following items: driver's license, state ID or birth certificate, proof of income or lack there of, proof of child care expense, rent receipts, utility and medical bills. Food stamps are only available to purchase food items, not paper or toiletries, clothes or shoes.

WIC

There is also a program called WIC (Women, Infant, and Children.) WIC is a federal assisted program of the Food and Nutrition Service of the United States Department of Agriculture. This program provides health care and nutrition for low-income families, pregnant women, breast feeding women, and infants and children under the age of five. Applicants must be residents in the state in which they apply. They must have income at or below an income level or standard set by the state agency or be determined automatically income-eligible. Applicants must be seen by a health professional such as a physician, nurse, or nutritionist who must determine whether the individual is at nutrition risk.

Mommies, if you are approved for WIC you may receive a monthly check, or voucher, and even more recently an EBT card. The food items provided by WIC are juice (single strength), milk, breakfast cereal, cheese, eggs, fruits and vegetables, whole wheat bread, fish (canned), legumes (dry or canned), and peanut butter. The program also provides tofu, soy milk, and medical foods for children and women with various metabolic or other diseases. You see, there is no reason why you and your little bundle of joy can't eat healthy balanced meals everyday. The help is out there, so no excuses.

Paternal Support

The child's father has a financial responsibility as well and you need to contact him for assistance. If he is willing to help, that makes the situation a lot better. If he is one who feels he doesn't have to participate, please contact your local attorney general's office and immediately apply for child support. This is not a matter of the heart or an act of revenge, but out of necessity. If you can't make him assist you, the state can. You didn't make this baby by yourself, so you shouldn't have to take care of this baby by yourself. This is not to imply that all men are bad parents, I just happen to know first hand that there are some who refuse to assume responsibility. I hope your baby has the type of father who is supportive and willing to go the extra mile to make sure both mommy and baby are fine.

Employment Options

A part-time job may be a consideration, if you are in need of additional income to make ends meet. There are plenty of companies that hire teens 15 years and older. Inquire at fast food restaurants and grocery stores. A grocery store would be ideal, because the employee discount you receive can provide more food for your household. Maybe even try a baby retail store. Again, the employee discount will be of great benefit for your toddler's needs because baby clothes and accessories can be really expensive. Places like Super Walmart and Super Target are also great employment prospects. They offer one-stop shopping and cover all the bases. They sell food, adult and baby clothes, toiletries, hardware and all your household needs, and don't forget about the fabulous employee discount. Finding a job that has multiple benefits will help ease some of the financial burden.

Also check to see if the employer offers medical insurance to part-time employees. Who knows, it just might be affordable for you. We have to make sure we cross all our t's and dot our i's. You never know all your options unless you ask. You have to exert smart and practical thinking.

Job Hunting Essentials: Application, Resume and Cover Letter

When filling out an application make sure all your information is accurate. Write legibly so there's no confusion for the employer. Some companies only accept applications online. If you don't have a computer, visit your local library and apply for a library card. This will give you access to their computers. Always provide references of good moral character on your application; people who operate with a high degree of integrity. Try a church member or maybe your school counselor.

If you've never had a job, volunteer work, school clubs or participation in community organizations serve as viable substitutes for previous employment. If you absolutely have no work history or affiliations, enter N/A for not-applicable. It is always a really good idea to have a resume and cover letter. It doesn't matter how big or small the job is, it's very important to always be professional. If you don't know how to develop a resume I have included two samples for you to model: one for a teen with job history, and one for the teen with no job history along with a sample cover letter.

Again, if you don't have a computer, make use of your local public library or even the computer lab at your school. After you have completed your resume and cover letter, ask someone to proofread it and check for spelling, grammatical and punctuation errors and feedback. A second set of eyes never hurts; because employers notice errors right away and that may hurt your chances of getting an interview.

Answering Machine Etiquette

Let's say your application and resume grab the attention of an employer and they call to schedule an interview. First, make sure your voice mail has a standard and professional greeting. Avoid music tones, and unprofessional speaking. An example of a professional greeting would be, *"You have reached the voice mail of your name, please leave your name, number, and a brief message and I will get back to you at my earliest convenience. Thanks and have a nice day."*

Resume For Teen with Work History

FIRST AND LAST NAME

Street Address   Home Phone
City, State Zip, Code   Cell Phone
                                                 Email Address

OBJECTIVES

(EXAMPLE: To obtain a position, in which I can bring to your organization enthusiasm, dedication, responsibility, and good work ethic, combined with a desire to utilize my skills.)

PROFESSIONAL EXPERIENCE

Company Name City, State   Start/End Date
Job Title
- Job Duty (example: Assisted customers with sales purchases).
- Job Duty.
- Job Duty.
- Job Duty.

Company Name City, State   Start/End Date
Job Title
- Job Duty (example: Assisted customers with sales purchases)
- Job Duty.
- Job Duty.
- Job Duty.
- Job Duty.

EDUCATION AND TRAINING

Student – Name of you School – City, State and Year you will graduate.

SKILLS INCLUDE: List all your skills. (Example: any computer software (like excel, or word), typing, filing, email, etc.)

Resume For Teen without Work History

FIRST AND LAST NAME

Street Address
City, State Zip, Code

Home Phone
Cell Phone
Email Address

OBJECTIVES

(EXAMPLE: To obtain a position, in which I can bring to your organization enthusiasm, dedication, responsibility, and good work ethic, combined with a desire to utilize my skills.)

EXPERIENCE

Volunteer Site Name City, State   Start/End Date
Job Title
- Job Duty (example: Assisted customers with sales purchases).
- Job Duty.
- Job Duty.
- Job Duty.

School and Club Name City, State   Start/End Date
Job Title
- Job Duty (example: Assisted customers with sales purchases)
- Job Duty.
- Job Duty.
- Job Duty.
- Job Duty.

EDUCATION AND TRAINING

Student – Name of you School – City, State and Year you will graduate.

SKILLS INCLUDE: List all your skills. (Example: any computer software (like excel, or word), typing, filing, email, etc.)

Cover Letter for Entry Level Position

Your Street Address
Your City, state, zip

Date

Person's Name
Company Name
Company Address
City, State, Zip

Dear (Mr./ Ms. Person's Name or Human Resources)

I am interested in an entry-level position with your company. I enclose my resume as a first step in exploring the possibilities of employment with (Company Name).

My most recent experience has been as a (previous positon title, or Volunteer, or school club name member) at (previous company name, volunteer organization name, or school name). I am/was responsible for the (major job description), in the company. In addition, I (another major job description).

I am currently enrolled in my (Grade) year at (school name). I plan to receive my diploma in (year). With a position with your company, I will gain the hands-on experience I need to ensure a strong work experience and ethic in a future career.

Thank you for taking your time to review my resume. I would certainly value the opportunity to meet with you and discuss how my skills would meet the needs of your company. Looking forward to hearing from you.

Sincerely,

(Your Name)

For an employer to call and have to sit and listen to five minutes of music playing before they can even leave a message, at best, is annoying and can be a deterrent. This can actually result in the employer hanging up and eliminating you as an interview candidate. Use good judgment in this area.

Interview Preparation

Now it's time for the interview. Always try to arrive at least 20 minutes early. Do not bring anyone with you. If you had to get a ride from someone, ask them to remain in the car or come back within a half hour. Dress professionally. If you don't have a suit, you can always wear slacks or a skirt and a nice blouse. Avoid bright and loud colors. Wear closed toe shoes; they're more professional. Make sure your appearance is neat and clean. Take a couple copies of your resume just in case the employer misplaced the ones you sent. Don't be nervous. Look at it from the perspective of you interviewing them to make sure their company is a suitable working environment for you as opposed to them interviewing you.

Stand up when the interviewer approaches you. Have a firm hand shake and look them directly in the eyes. This let's them know your serious. Smile and speak intelligently. Sit up straight, no slouching. Do not chew gum. Make sure your cell phone is turned off. Avoid words like "well" and "um" before a sentence.

Some questions employers ask during interviews are: Tell me about yourself. Your response should be, *"I'm a student at (school name), and my past experiences have been in (list previous job fields, school clubs, and any volunteer work)."*

Q. Why do you think you will be right for this position?

A. *"I have significant experience in (name several duties)."*

Q. What is your greatest weakness?

A. *"I have had trouble in the past with being a perfectionist and sometimes that can slow me down."*

Q. What is Your Greatest Strength?

A. *"My time management skills are excellent. I am organized, efficient, and take pride in excelling at my work."*

Q. Are you a team player?

A. *"Yes, I'm very much a team player. In fact, I've had opportunities in my school to develop my skills as a team player, such as on team projects and group assignments."*

Q. Where do you see yourself in the future?

A. *"I see myself progressing in (the company name), learning new skills to the benefit of (the company name), as well as obtaining a bachelors degree in (college major)."*

You should also be prepared to ask the employer questions, such as,

"Describe the typical responsibilities of the position."

"Will I receive any formal training?"

"Are there opportunities for advancement within the organization?"

"What are the hours?"

"When can I expect to hear from you?"

When the interview is over, always thank the employer for taking out the time to interview you. It's also a nice gesture to send a thank you card. It keeps you on their minds.

Child care options

Let's say you get the job. Now who is going to take care of the baby while you're at work? This would be a good time to reach out to family and friends. I was fortunate; my mother didn't work, so she watched my son for me while I was at work and school. You may not have that luxury, so you might have to find some child care assistance. The ideal is if you know someone with a home day care that's not too expensive. You could manage the cost out of your paycheck.

If not, here is what you need to do. Check and see if there is a child care resource and referral agency (CCR&R) in the area where you live. They may have information about child care programs with special funding options or sliding fee scales. Links to State CCR&R agencies are available on the NCCIC web site at *http://nccic.acf.hhs.gov/statedata/dirs/display.cfm?title=ccr*

You can also contact Child Care Aware, a free, federally-funded service, at *www.childcareaware.org* or via phone at 800-424-2246 to find a local CCR&R.

Savings Save

When you finally have the baby situated in day care and have been on your job a few months, you need to open up a savings account for you and your baby. I know what you're thinking. I don't have enough money for a savings account let alone two. Just hear me out. At some banks it only takes $20 to open an account. If you have to open yours one month and the baby's another that's okay. Since you're working, see if your employer offers direct deposit. This will eliminate check cashing fees and standing in long lines.

On pay day withdraw all the money you need to pay bills and buy home necessities. Each time leave $10 in the account from that pay check and put $5 into your baby's account. I know it doesn't seem like much, but over time it will add up. Later down the road when your pay increases, you will be able to increase your deposits.

Mommies, it's all about baby steps. I know it's going to be hard, but try not to spend the money you're saving. Things may come up where you don't have a choice, just try and replace it. Learning to save money is setting the foundation for a secure future.

Treat Yourself

If after you have paid all your bills, and have everything you need in the house, buy something special for yourself. It doesn't have to be expensive. If could be a shirt you saw on sale or even a pair of earrings. You have to do something that makes you feel good or else it will all seem in vain. Just don't go over board. I mean don't spend your last on an outfit when you know the light bill needs to be paid. In due time, you will have everything you want, it just takes a little work.

Budgeting 101

To make sure you keep tabs on your finances, purchase a calendar; nothing expensive. It can be a cheap one you can hang on your wall. On the calendar, write down all your paydays. Then write down the days that the bills are due. Here is an example.

Dreams Altered BUT NOT *Abandoned*

Thursday	Friday
Oct 1	Oct 2
Payday	Cell Bill- $68.23
Light Bill- $89.00	Daycare - $50.00
Water Bill- $30.00	

This way you won't forget to pay the bills, and you won't have to worry about having your utilities and services cut off. It will also be a good idea to create a spread sheet listing all of your bills, with the account numbers, web site addresses, and your login and password if you pay them on line. For example, see below:

Bill	Account#	Website	Login	Password
Lights	123456	www.com	aaaa	111111
Water	s416484	www.com	bbbb	222222
Cell	6436456	www.com	cccc	333333

To streamline some of your expenses, select a downgraded cable package. You don't have to have HBO. Turn lights off in rooms when no one is in them. Try not to waste water. Limit your showers to 3-5 minutes. While brushing your teeth, don't let the water run. Cook instead of eating out. It can be very expensive and is not often very healthy. Sometimes you're going to want to hang out with your friends and maybe go to a movie or something. That's alright occasionally, but don't make a habit of it. The price of movie tickets and outside entertainment will definitely put a dent in your pocket. Why not host game night at your house instead? Or maybe rent a movie from the local video store and invite friends over. You will also save money on gas this way. Have you seen the price of gas lately? Pretty soon everyone will have to ride a bike to work. Again, you have options, but it's up to you which ones you choose. I hope you choose wisely.

five

Balancing School Work and Baby

Mommies, you now have a lot on your plate. It's time to learn how to balance it all. This can be quite challenging, especially since there are only 24-hours in a day. Here's how you can stretch those 24-hour days.

It all begins with planning. In the previous chapter, I mentioned purchasing a calendar to set bill reminders. Well I suggest you do to the same to manage your time. If you don't want to use another calendar, you may prefer a day planner. You can find them at any major retailer. The average cost for a planner ranges anywhere between $9.00 and $25.00. If that expense is not a current budget item, you have the option to create one on the computer. This way nothing will be forgotten or overlooked because you have ten million items on your plate. *(See the planner example below.)*

Appointments	Time	To Do
	7am	Take baby to daycare
		School
Math work due	8am	"
		"
	9am	"
		"
Dr. appointment	10am	"
		"
	11am	"
		"
	12pm	Work
		"
	1pm	"
		"
	2pm	"
		"
	3pm	"
		"
	4pm	"
		Pick up the baby
	5pm	Cook
		Eat/ Fed baby
	6pm	Bathe baby
		Put baby to sleep
	7pm	Clean up
		Do homework
	8pm	

Dreams Altered BUT NOT Abandoned

Have a Plan or Plan to be Frantic

Try planning out your schedule at least a week in advance, this way you will stay caught up on everything. Including homework assignment due dates to your planner is an added idea. Try to be proactive by completing and turning in assignments ahead of time. When you are a parent, you never know when you may encounter emergencies that cause you to miss work or school. Staying ahead of the game eliminates your falling behind and wards off undue stress. We all know how difficult it is to catch up on school work while completing present assignments.

Your planner should also list all doctor appointments for both you and your baby so you won't be charged cancellations fees as a result of forgotten or missed appointments.

Plan the Housework

It's also a good idea to incorporate your chores into your planner so that you are more likely to get them done rather than putting them off. This method, for some reason, is less stressful. I can testify that it worked for me. When planning out your chores, try not to overwhelm yourself by doing too much all at one time. You don't want to wear yourself out. Cleaning your home may not be a lot of fun, but it is definitely required, especially when you have a child. It is necessary to keep as much dirt, grime, and bacteria away from them as possible.

Picking up as you go will eliminate a lot of cleaning time. I found it easier to do housework while my baby was asleep. Your toddler may be one who is content sitting in the playpen with toys. That's all good; just make sure they are in the same room with you, so you can keep an eye on them while you work. If you tend to use strong scented cleaners, it's better to wait until they're napping or in bed for the evening. Try doing laundry on your off days. Mop, sweep, and vacuum once a week, unless sooner or more frequent is deemed necessary. Accidents and spills will happen, and keeping the floor clean is very important because babies are notorious for picking things up and putting them in their mouths.

Sanitize your bathroom once or even twice a week. Try ironing all your clothes for the week on the weekend or your day(s) off. I know it sounds like a lot of work, but it adds time to your week, when you don't have to go home every day and iron. I still iron all my clothes for the week on Sunday so I can benefit from my free time during the week.

Plan Your Meals

You may want to try this with cooking also. Cook a variety of meats on your day off, and during the week all you have to do is add your vegetables and other side items. These suggestions are major time savers. Hopefully you'll do better than I did. I wanted to eat cereal everyday for dinner. Mommies, we know that is not healthy, but I eventually learned my lesson.

Here are a few good simple meals suggestions. Try grilled chicken breast with vegetables. If you don't like grilled chicken you can always bake or fry it. Baked is the healthier and preferred choice. Try baked fish and a potato. Spaghetti and meat sauce is also pretty easy. Tacos are easy and quite inexpensive. There are a ton of dinner choices, just pick and choose based on your food preferences and ease of preparation.

Plan Baby Time

Don't forget to add time with your baby on your planner. It is imperative that you spend quality time with your child; as much as possible. As they get a little older, they don't sleep as much, so you need to occupy their time. Some of the most inexpensive things that you can do with your baby tend to be the most fun.

You can go to your local library and check out age appropriate books to read to your baby and it doesn't cost you anything. This is something you can actually start doing from day one. If you start reading to your baby when they are really young it helps them to become good readers. A stroll in the park on weather permitting days is also another cost effective, yet fun activity for both you and baby. There's nothing like good old fresh air mixed with great exercise for mommy. Visit the local pet store or maybe even the zoo. Babies get so excited when they see animals. There is usually a fee for entrance to the zoo, but the pet store is an ample substitute and free of charge unless you make a purchase.

If you have friends who are also mommies, schedule a play date. This serves a two-fold purpose; while the babies are at play, mommy girlfriends can use this time to catch up. You can also sit in the middle of your living room floor and play games like patty cake or peek-a-boo. And for those times when you are just too worn out, and those times will come, all you have to do is turn on the television to an animated show. That always catches baby's attention. Get real comfy on the couch, sit there and rub your baby's back while you watch television together. Your baby will still be provided with their much needed attention through touch while you get some much needed rest all at the same time.

Plan Mommy Time

Last but not least, always try and schedule your "me" time on the planner as well. It's essential; actually critical for your well-being and your sanity. How many times do you run like crazy doing this and doing that without taking time out to do something you enjoy? It happens all the time. Between school, work, and taking care of your baby, self can sometimes get lost in the shuffle. My motto is, *"How can you take care of someone else if you're not taking care of yourself?"*

If it's only 30 minutes of unused time out of the day, I suggest you take it. You'll soon find out that you can do a lot with 30 minutes. Once the baby is a sleep and you're done with everything else, take a nice relaxing bath with candlelight and soft music. Try not to fall asleep in the tub; I don't want you to drown. You may want to get in a little television and even on a good day maybe rent a movie.

> **❝How can you take care of someone else if you're not taking care of yourself.❞**

Another good idea is to buy a diary. If a diary is too expensive, a regular note book will do just fine. Sometimes it helps to ease stress by writing out your thoughts and events of the day. A release of all the negative energy is a must and journaling is a great alternative if you don't have anyone to talk to. Spend time reading your bible. It may be confusing at first, but the more you read the more you'll understand. Since this time is for yourself, write out goals you want to accomplish. This is the perfect time while there are no distractions and you can think clearly.

Take this time and give yourself a manicure and pedicure. When you start making more money you can treat yourself and have them done professionally. Maybe you can rearrange your bedroom. Sometimes recreating your space will give you a sense of clarity and newness. Also try finding a baby sitter every now and then, so that you can get out of the house. I'm sure you feel like the four walls are closing in on you. Walk around the mall with friends or if the budget permits, see a movie or grab a bite to eat. Once you've finally had that much needed time for yourself, you will once again be able to tackle the world with vigor and a reassured confidence.

Reserving me time made a world of difference. It felt like I recharged my batteries. Once I was back into mommy mode, I was able to be super mom again, but with a refreshed attitude and spirit.

Continue Your Education

Okay little mama, now is the time to work on getting your degree. I know you're exhausted and you really don't feel like returning to school for another four years, but guess what? You're going. I probably sound like your mom right about now, but I have so much faith in you and I know you're going to be successful. I'm here to give you all the moral support and encouragement you need. Expanding your education beyond high school expands your possibilities and presents a million more chances for better career opportunities.

The day my mother and I went down to the local community college and registered me for school, I was so proud of myself. I felt like I was beating all the odds and limitations that everyone else placed on me. I couldn't believe that I was actually going to be a college student after all. I beamed with pride and I knew I was setting a good example for my baby. I was moving forward, and no one was going to stop me. So chin up, chest out, and let's get going.

Visit Your Guidance Counselor

When you begin your senior year of high school, schedule an appointment with your school counselor to discuss college options and seek advice and direction. Prior to your visit, compile a list of schools you are interested in. If you haven't already done so, visit some of the campuses and talk with students, professors, and counselors at those schools. Request information regarding admissions requirements, financial aid, and corresponding deadlines. If you haven't decided on a major, don't let that be a deterrent, you can always start out taking the core curriculum.

Your counselor can provide you with information about schools in your immediate area, and assist you with all you need to have accomplished before you graduate, so you will be ready to move forward. It's also a good idea to ask your counselor about classes you can take in high school that may also be offered at the college level. This way you can earn college credits and get a head start on the classes you have to take in college.

College Aptitude Tests

Register for and take the ACT, SAT Reasoning and SAT Subject Tests; along with any other tests required for admission to the colleges to which you are applying. If you have difficulty paying the registration fee(s), see your guidance counselor and inquire about fee waivers.

How Will I Pay for College?

College can be very expensive, so if you are not able to afford tuition, and may not be a candidate for academic scholarship, don't worry; you still have options.

Two-year Community College

A two-year community college is an alternative and a lot less expensive. A community college offers classes that will meet your first two years requirements at a four-year university. They may also offer some of the required electives needed for your major.

Financial Assistance Options

Financial Aid is another option for financial assistance in the form of grants, scholarships, loans, or paid employment (work study) to assist with college expenses. These programs are funded from various sources to distribute more than $100 billion per year in assistance. They may cover lab fees, books, and other course-related fees. The Robert C. Byrd Honors Scholarship Program Education Dashboard gives money to state education agencies to award scholarships to graduating high school seniors. Each state education agency has its own application and deadline.

To find your state agency's web site, visit the address listed below: *http://wdcrobcolp01.ed.gov/Programs /EROD/org_list.cfm?category_ID=SHE.*

FAFSA

If you decide to apply for financial aid instead, you can visit *www.fafsa.ed.gov* to complete the application. If you need assistance with filling out your application, which is called a FAFSA, ask your high school counselor for assistance or contact the Federal Student Aid Information Center at (800) 4-FED-AID (800) 433-3243, (319) 337-5665 or contact the TTY line for the hearing impaired at (800) 730-8913.

You should complete the FASFA application in the beginning of your senior year, so be sure to search the web site for application deadlines. You will need the following information and documents prior to filling out your FASFA application: social security card (number), driver's license (if applicable), w-2 forms and other records of earned wages, previous year federal income tax return; or your parents previous year federal income tax return (if you are a dependent student), current bank statements, and alien registration or permanent resident card (if you are not a U.S. citizen).

When filling out your FASFA, you need to also apply for a PIN. A PIN is a 4-digit number used in combination with your social security number, name, and date of birth to identify you as someone who has access rights to your personal information on Federal Student Aid web sites. The application process is much easier if you use your PIN to sign your application electronically. After you have submitted your FASFA you can access your application status at any time, but it is recommended to allow at least one week after submission before checking your status if you used a PIN to sign your application. If you made any errors on your application, you will have to wait until it is processed before making corrections. Corrections can be made online through the corrections portal of the web site.

Other Cost Cutting Ideas

Here are some other tips and suggestions for ways to cut down on some of the college expenses. Purchasing used books instead of new ones is a great money saver. You may consider applying for a part-time job on campus. Who knows you may receive discounts at the bookstore or other campus-related resources. Purchase a five-subject notebook and use it for all your classes, as opposed to investing in a separate notebook for each class. I'm sure there is a plethora of other ways to cut costs; just remember to think smart, not hard.

Applying for College

Now you're ready to apply for college. The studentaid.ed.gov web site explains that *"applying to schools means more than just filling out forms. You need to understand each school's requirements, gather information, meet deadlines, and pay any necessary fees for each submitted application."*

When you complete your college admissions applications, make sure you follow all instructions carefully and pay particular attention to application deadlines. At least two weeks before the deadline, ask your counselor and teachers to submit all requested documents to the college, such as grade transcripts and letters of recommendation. Make sure the admissions offices at each school have received your application material along with any additional documents that needed to accompany the application. Your applications need to be correct and submitted on time so they'll be processed quickly.

Contact the financial aid offices at those schools to ensure they are in receipt of everything they need from you. You will start to receive responses from the schools you applied to in the early spring. Compare the acceptance offers, acceptance letters and financial aid/scholarship offers before making a final decision.

Accuplacer Testing and Class Registration

Once admission is completed, you will be required to meet with an advisor and possibly requested to take an accuplacer test. The accuplacer test is an assessment of your academic skills in math, English, and reading, so that you can be properly placed. Once you have completed the test, a score report will be created. Your college advisor will then go over the test results with you and let you know if you are required to enroll in any developmental classes for math, English, and reading.

Once you have gone over test scores and requirements with an advisor you need to register for your classes. It's a good idea to review the course catalog in advance so that you have an idea of what is available. As I stated earlier, if you're undecided about your major, that's okay, you can still register for your college core curriculum classes. These classes usually include two semesters of English, science, history, political science, and maybe a foreign language. It also includes one semester of math, physical education, humanities, computer science, visual and performing arts, literature, and understanding the human community.

If you are required to enroll in any of the developmental classes, they must be taken before you can enroll for the college level coursework for that

"Expanding your education beyond high school expands your possibilities and presents a million more chances for better career opportunities. "

department. Taking your core classes in the beginning allows you to devote time to your college major in the final semesters. Check all class times and register for classes that don't interfere with your work schedule or your baby. It's important to get your classes as close together as possible. This will eliminate you having to leave school and return at a later time.

Balance harder classes with easier ones. Don't register classes together that require a great deal of paper writing, because you'll be overwhelmed, and faced with major frustration. You also shouldn't register for all easy classes in the beginning, because then you'll have to fight through all the harder classes in the end.

You may want to mix online classes with on-campus classes for even more of a life balance. Most colleges offer some sort of distance learning. Online classes help free up your schedule, but require discipline. You must be responsible and accountable to log on to retrieve assignments and due dates. Just be reminded that some online classes require a visit to the on-site campus center for testing, so make sure you are able to comply.

If certain required classes aren't available, ask your advisor if there are other classes you can take that would substitute for the class you're not able to attend. In most cases, there are several options for alternates. Once you have finally registered for your classes, make sure you add the days and times to your planner as we discussed in the balancing work, home, school, and baby chapter.

College Life

College is a lot different from high school; there isn't going to be anyone making sure you get there on time, or that you're doing your homework assignments. If you don't turn in an assignment, that's just on you, along with a big fat zero (0) recorded as your grade. Bear in mind if you are receiving financial aid, you're only allowed to miss so many days before they take it away from you, and possibly require you to pay it back. So let that be a deciding factor before you choose to miss a day of school.

Do everything in your power to be successful. Stay in contact with all of your professors; let them know of any issues or concerns you may have. If there is ever an opportunity for extra credit, do it even if you don't need it. It will be to your benefit and reinforce your becoming a dedicated student.

Always arrive on time for class; if possible arrive a little early. There is nothing worse than walking into class late in the middle of a lecture.

You will receive a syllabus at the beginning of each semester for all your classes with the outline of the course along with course assignments and due dates, so try and work pro actively and complete assignments way ahead of time. Always take good and legible notes. I stress legible, because there were occasions when I got home from class and started to study, I wasn't able to read my own writing. That was what I considered to be a huge waste of time. If you happen to have a small tape recorder, ask your professor if they permit taping of lectures, this way you won't miss a thing.

To ensure that you are prepared for tests and quizzes, have someone else quiz you to see how well you know the material. While studying take short breaks to allow your brain time to process and retain the information. It's not a bad idea to join a study group. Try and get at least eight hours sleep every night and eat well balanced healthy meals.

With college life also come college parties. Now look mommies, you know you have other responsibilities, so keep the parties to a minimum. If you just have to go to one, make sure you get your studying and school work done during the week, so that you don't fall behind, because you decided that you just couldn't miss the party that everyone is attending. Don't let other people distract you and get you off course. Sometimes friends can be your worst enemies. If they are not focused and on track, they will easily persuade you and get you off track. Remember the old saying, *"Misery loves company."*

Well, you are coming along quite nicely. I'm so proud of you. You could have given up but you chose not to. Continuing your education is one of the smartest choices you could ever make. Just watch how successful you will be and remember, I told you so. For every obstacle that may hinder your progress or have the potential to block your path, you have the power, strength, and the courage to overcome with the help of God, and don't you ever forget it.

Proactive Prevention

Prevention is not limited to the idea of protection from pregnancy. Prevention begins prior to the teenage season in a girl's life. I would like to introduce some proactive measures that may contribute to the success of the life a teen girl. A healthy approach in these vital areas may redefine prevention as a proactive investment in the life of a young girl that can prevent them from prematurely participating in activities that can eventually lead to teen pregnancy.

Fathers and Daughters

Fathers need to assume more of an active role in the lives of their daughters. Dads, date your daughters. Okay, get your mind out of the gutter; I'm not implying anything inappropriate. Children learn by example, so demonstrate to your daughter how a man treats a woman. Her first point of reference is how you treat her mother. Be intentional about spending quality time with your daughter. Take her to dinner at a nice restaurant. Be the gentleman; open and hold the doors, and pull out her chair. **Talk with her**; find out who she is and what she's thinking. **Esteem her**; let her know how proud she makes you. **Compliment her**; tell her how beautiful she is. **Secure her**; and ensure that you'll always be there for her.

When a teenage girl has the love and support of her father, she is less likely to fall for the one-liners and believe any and everything some young guy who seems interested tells her. She's already accustomed to receiving positive attention, so what ever little Romeo tries to sell her is not so easily bought for lack of love, affirmation or self-esteem.

Young men can appear to be quite charming and debonair; they'll open and hold the door, real gentleman-like or even pull out the chair, while the motive may be to woo, win and "hit the skins". But your little lady will appreciate the gesture while holding firm to her positive convictions of self-value, esteem and worth.

When she's secure in self, she won't settle for anything less than being respected as a young lady, because she now has a point of reference and positive experiences to draw from. She's not out looking for outside validations. More fathers need to affirm their little girls and assure and reassure them. Besides, you are the first man they will ever love or be loved by.

Fathers, help your girls build strong foundations in God. You are the head of the home, so embrace accountability as the head of the family, husband, father, spiritual lead, provider and disciplinarian. Partner with your wife to lay a solid foundation in God, so your family will be governed by biblical principles.

I'm writing this as I fight back tears. There are so many young girls who need their fathers but are without them and looking for substitutions of that male influence in their lives (i.e., looking for love in all the wrong places). I'm not overlooking all the great dads out there, I'm merely speaking out about the ones who are absent and much needed in the lives of their daughters. I personally applaud all of the fathers in the world who are active participants in the lives of their children. Thank you for doing your part.

Mothers and Daughters

Okay Mothers, don't think I'm letting you off the hook. Be mindful that everything your daughter sees you do, they are more than likely to repeat. You are their example of what womanhood looks like. Remember, your conduct is on display. Talk to your daughters about virtue, honor, reputation and character. Share with them your experiences and even the mistakes, so they don't have to repeat them.

Teach your daughter how to keep her body pure and carry and conduct herself as a lady. Insist upon modest dress (trendy and fashionable is fine, but without exposing all her body parts). Women who dress provocatively send a message of promiscuity to men. Set boundaries and guidelines for what is expected of her and follow up.

If you are a single mom, be mindful about bringing different men around your daughters. First, for obvious reasons; you can't be too liberal with allowing men access to your daughter. Second, your daughter will deem it acceptable to be with this guy, and that guy, and so on. She will follow the example you set. Third, you can't lead if you can't follow. Good advice is good, but it's even better when exhibited in the life of the person giving it; parents included. Lastly, being a single mom has its own set of challenges, and you don't want the same for your daughter.

Mothers, you must also set an example for how your daughter should be treated. When you allow men to mistreat you and behave abusively toward you, you give your daughter permission to emulate your behavior and accept physically abusive relationships and verbal disrespect.

Mothers, maintain an open line of communication with your daughter, this is vital. When a girl knows that she can go to her mommy with anything, she will never feel alone and won't hesitate to seek your guidance and advice.

If you just happen to be a young teen – mommy or not – who have never been told how beautiful you are, let me be the first to say,

"You are very beautiful and don't let anyone tell you differently."

Just Say "NO"

Now, having said all that, I'm going to keep it real mommies, the best way to not get pregnant the first, second, third or anytime is to just say NO. If you don't know how to say NO, don't worry, I will help you.

Afrikaans - GEEN	Italian – NO
Arabic – لا	Japanese – いいえ
Bulgarian – He	Korean –아무도
Chinese – 沒有	Lithuanian - NE
Czech – Ne	Persian – نخير
Dutch – NEE	Portuguese – نخير
English – No	Romanian – nr.
French – NON	Russian – HET
Greek – Αριθ.	Spanish – No
German – NEIN	Swahili - NO
Hebrew – פלסטיני	Swedish – NEJ
Hungarian – Nincs	Thai – ไม่มี
Indonesian – NO	Welsh - NA

Now you can say *"NO"* in 27 different languages; it can't get any clearer than that. Believe me, all jokes aside; I just want you to be informed. If you just so happen to run across that real smooth dude, with the velvety voice, the right swagger, dimpled cheek, sweet smile, who checked your frame, and looked at you like dessert, there is a one word solution. NO!!!

Don't fall for it. For the mommies, you already know the script. Yes, he may tell you how beautiful you are, and of course, he wants to get to know you better and you did notice that he's been checking you out from head to toe without making any eye contact. Come on now, we've been there, done that, bought the t-shirt, got the mug and the baby to prove it.

So, when Boy Wonder keeps laying it on thick, it's up to you to tell him *"NO"* in the language of your choice, Stay focused. The very last thing you need is another baby. You are already experiencing the challenges of raising one. Just tell him the truth; that you are a single mom, with a job, bills, and school with no time for a relationship. You can also add that maybe down the rode when you have accomplished your goals, you two can talk about hooking up. Is that what you girls still call it these days, hooking up? Okay, I have accepted that fact that I'm getting older, and I don't know all the latest lingo.

Getting back to the subject, some guys may back off, but you just might be dealing with Mr. Persistent, who really thinks he can break you down and coerce you into having sex with him. Don't do it. He is not worth sacrificing everything you have worked so hard to accomplish thus far. If he really cares about you he will understand, respect your decision and not interfere with or jeopardize your future.

Okay Mommy, this also applies to the father of your child. You may still be in a relationship with him, but you still need to tell him, "NO". Remember you have 27 to choose from. If he doesn't accept your decision, kick his behind to the curb. My bad, I know, I'll stop with the slang in a minute, but you do catch my drift. If you should find yourself in a situation where you have told the guy "NO" and he keeps trying, and you no longer know how to respond, below are a few sample rebuttals that you can use.

Guy: *"But baby you know I love you."*

Mommy: *"If you love me, you can wait for me."*

Guy: *"You're going to be my wife one day, why do we have to wait."*

Mommy: *"Because I'm not your wife now."*

Guy: *"Everybody is doing it."*

Mommy: *"Well I'm not everybody and you should realize that."*

Guy: *"If you won't have sex with me, I'll leave you."*

Mommy: *"See ya; that means that's all you wanted any way."*

Guy: *"I'll find someone that will have sex with me if you won't."*

Mommy: *"If you can go and be with someone else that easily, that means you didn't love me in the first place."*

Guy: *"It's not like you haven't had sex before, what's the problem."*

Mommy: *"The problem is that I already have one child; I don't need another one right now."*

Guy: *"No one will know."*

Mommy: *"Guess what? I will."*

Guy: *"You know you want it too."*

Mommy: *"No, what I want is a college education and to be the best mother that I can be."*

Guy: *"It will make our relationship stronger."*

Mommy: *"No, you respecting my decision will make our relationship stronger."*

The Company You Keep

Another approach to prevention is to choose your friends wisely. Surround yourself with positive people and friends who will tell you what you need to hear vs. what you want to hear. I'm talking about people who are working hard, and setting goals. These are the people you can learn a lot from.

Join a youth program in your church. Some churches even have child care centers. You can even join programs in your school. Maybe join a drama class, student council, or even the school paper. If that doesn't work you can always create your own program. You can start a food drive, for the less fortunate. This will also look good on a resume or college application. Join or even start a book club with some of the neighborhood girls or your classmates.

Why not form a study group? Don't just pick your friends; ask some of the really smart students to join. Try to stick with the same time and place so that there is a feeling of consistency. Find out what each person is good at so that you can divide the work evenly and no one feels overwhelmed. Find people who are committed. Forming a study group allows you to learn class material faster and complete class projects more quickly. It also helps to make new friends and network with other students.

It's really important for you to stay active. Having a bunch of time on your hands can sometimes cause people to make bad decisions and get involved with the wrong crowd. It's easy to be persuaded to do wrong when you don't have anything else to do; that's why I stress hanging around the right crowd.

I know you've heard the expression *"birds of a feather, flock together."* I know what your thinking, *"just because my friends are doing it, doesn't mean I'll do it."* That's true I'll admit that, but be realistic, how often have you done something only because your friends were doing it? Don't feel bad it's human nature at that age, so that's why it's important to pick and choose your friends wisely, because they have a lot of influence in your life. It's called *"peer pressure"* so why not have peers that pressure you to do the *"right thing."*

If you have friends who are out there having sex with God knows who or what, naturally they will influence you to do the same. Let me tell you, *"It's not a good look."* Let your friends know that you're at a point in your life where you have to re-channel your focus and keep your priorities straight. Tell them that you're doing everything in your power not to get pregnant again. They may call you weak or other foolish names, but in the end, they'll be the ones looking foolish. If they do call you names, you may realize they were never your friends at all. A true friend will always give you good sound advice; never advice that will bring you hurt or harm.

When you stand your ground and show unshakable confidence, you'll avoid making bad decisions, so make sure you maintain high levels of self-esteem. Everything negative that was ever said or done to you, turn it around and make it your building blocks to help take you to higher destinations. It's not going to be easy, but in the end you will live down all the negative press – all the people who said you would never be anything; the ones who laughed at you behind your back and the ones who said you weren't pretty enough, or talented enough.

Every time a block is tossed your way, don't even acknowledge it, just take the block and place it under your feet. Pretty soon all the blocks that were thrown your way will have you standing high enough to just pull down your dreams. When you look down, you'll see all the haters at the bottom who provided your blocks. You don't have to throw it back in their faces, just smile and say thank you for helping me turn your blocks into my stepping stones.

I know this is going to sound corny, but every morning when you wake up, look in the mirror and say to yourself, *"No matter what anyone says, I am beautiful inside and out. And thank you God for taking the time to uniquely create me."*

Teen Pregnancy Prevention Programs

Teen pregnancy and childbearing bring substantial social and economic costs through immediate and long-term impacts on teen parents and their children.

The Centers for Disease Control

The Centers for Disease Control (CDC) Division of Reproductive Health, Adolescent Reproductive Health program promotes sexual and reproductive health among adolescents and young adults with a primary focus on youth facing disparities and high rates of unintended pregnancy. Through partnerships and capacity building, they accomplished their mission by translating science into practice to reduce sexual risk behaviors and promote healthy youth development.

- Increasing the numbers of teens receiving evidence-based or evidence-informed teen pregnancy prevention programs, including youth development and curriculum-based programs that reduce risk factors associated with teen pregnancy.

- Linking teens to quality health services by strengthening linkages between teen pregnancy prevention programs and community-based clinical services.

- Educating stakeholders (community leaders, parents and other constituents) about relevant evidence-based or evidence-informed strategies to reduce teen pregnancy and data on needs and resources in target communities.

- Supporting the sustain ability of the community wide teen pregnancy prevention effort.

- Supporting the exchange of information among scientific and program colleagues, partners, and the public.

In 2001, approximately one-half of pregnancies in the United States were unintended (Finer 2006, Perspectives on Sexual and Reproductive Health), and the United States has set a national goal of decreasing unintended pregnancies to 30% by 2010.

Efforts to decrease unintended pregnancy include finding better forms of contraception, and increasing contraceptive use and adherence. Research has also focused on better understanding pregnancy intention and how it is measured. As one study suggests, *"A better understanding of the multiple dimensions of unintended pregnancy also may lead to a better understanding of the consequences of these pregnancies"*

The President's Teen Pregnancy Prevention Initiative

As part of the President's Teen Pregnancy Prevention Initiative, (TPPI), CDC is partnering with the Office of Public Health and Science (OPHS) to reduce teenage pregnancy and address disparities in teen pregnancy and birth rates. The OPHS Office of Adolescent Health *"http://www.hhs.gov/ophs/oah/prevention/research/programs/index.html."* (OAH) is supporting public and private entities to fund medically accurate and age appropriate evidence-based or innovative program models to reduce teen pregnancy. The purpose of this program is to demonstrate the effectiveness of innovative, multi-component, community wide initiatives in reducing rates of teen pregnancy and births in communities with the highest rates, with a focus on reaching African American and Latino/Hispanic youth aged 15–19. A community wide model is an intervention implemented in defined communities (specified geographic area) applying a common approach with different strategies. Community wide approaches will be tailored to the specified community, and will include broad-based strategies that reach a majority of youth in the community (e.g., through communication strategies and media campaigns); and intensive strategies reaching youth most in need of prevention programming (e.g., through implementation of evidence-based programs and improved links to services).

Program goals are—

- Reduce the rates of pregnancies and births to youth in the target areas.

- Increase youth access to evidence-based and evidence-informed programs to prevent teen pregnancy.

Increase linkages between teen pregnancy prevention programs and community-based clinical services.

Youth outcomes:

- Reduce teen birth rates by 10% in targeted communities;

- Reduce teen pregnancies in targeted communities;

- Increase the percentage of youth who abstain from or delay sexual intercourse; and

- Increase the consistent and correct use of condoms and other effective methods of contraception among sexually active youth.

eight

All About Birth Control

Abstinence

Again, I want to reiterate that the only 100% *"sure"* and *"safe"* method of birth control is abstinence. I understand that this notion isn't the top ranking item in the people's popular opinion poll, but it is the truth. It is also the Godly way.

In addition to abstaining removing any chance of pregnancy, it totally eliminates the threat of coming in contact with or contracting any of a host of sexually transmitted diseases.

Ladies, I understand the curiosities, peer pressure, social popularity and the overall emphasis on sex in our culture, but celibacy is still popular among young people and there are many who find value in keeping themselves until marriage.

In the case of our teens who are already Mommies, you can't get back your virginity, but you can make a decision to return to purity, which gives you the opportunity to make all things new. When the physical pressures are removed, you can experience so much more from your interactions in relationships of all kinds and take the limits off.

For informational purposes, below is a compiled list of birth control methods that can be found on the US Department of Health and Human Services web site. It's complete with tips, statistics, and usage instructions.

The Basics of Contraception

Know the Facts:

What is contraception?

Contraception (also known as birth control) refers to the many different methods of preventing pregnancy. The latex condom is the only contraceptive method that may provide protection against some STDs, including HIV/AIDS. Research shows that latex condoms may not be effective against some STDs such as Human Papilloma Virus (HPV - the virus that causes genital warts.)

Who needs contraception?

Anyone who has sex and doesn't want to get pregnant or get someone pregnant needs contraception. Any time you have sex, there is a risk of pregnancy.

Are some methods of contraception better than others at preventing pregnancy?

Yes. If you choose to have sex, know that some contraception methods are more effective than others, but no other method offers you total assurance. To be effective, whatever method you choose must be used correctly and consistently. Always read and follow the package instructions. It is a good idea to discuss this with your health provider.

Is the condom the only kind of contraception for males?

No. Vasectomy is a permanent method of contraception. But the condom is the most common method used by young males. Remember, the condom not only protects you from getting (or getting someone) pregnant, it may also provide protection against HIV/AIDS and some other STDs.

How do I decide which method of contraception to use?

Your health care provider can help you decide which method is best for you. Remember, even if you are using a method like the pill, the latex condom is the only method that may provide some protection against HIV/AIDS and some STDs.

Do I need a prescription to get contraception?

Latex condoms can be purchased without a prescription, but other methods require one. Even if you use a nonprescription method, it is a good idea to see a health care provider on a regular basis.

How much protection do contraceptive methods provide against all STDs, including HIV/AIDS?

Most contraceptive methods do not protect against STDs, including HIV/AIDS. But latex condoms may provide some protection. Without a latex condom, STDs can be passed from person to person during vaginal, oral, or anal sex. While some STDs are curable, others are not. Even when another form of contraception is used, it is important to also use a latex condom to provide as much protection as possible.

Male Condom

What is it?
A thin film sheath placed over the erect penis to stop sperm from reaching the egg.

How do I use it?
- Put it on the erect penis right before sex.
- Use it only once and then throw it away.
- Pull out before the penis softens.
- Hold the condom against the base of the penis before you pull out.

How do I get it?
- You do not need a prescription.
- You can buy it over-the-counter.

Possibility of getting pregnant
- (Number of pregnancies expected per 100 women who use this method for one year)
- Out of 100 women who use this method, 11-16 may get pregnant.
- The most important thing is that you use a condom every time you have sex.

Some Risks
- Irritation
- Allergic reactions (If you are allergic to latex, you can try condoms made of polyurethane.)

Does it protect me from sexually transmitted infections (STIs)?
- Except for abstinence, latex condoms are the best protection against HIV/AIDS and other STIs.
- Condoms are the only contraceptive product that may protect against most sexually transmitted infections (STIs).

Female Condom

What is it?
A lubricated, thin polyurethane pouch that is put into the vagina.

How do I use it?
- Put the female condom into the vagina right before sex.
- Use it only once and then throw it away.
- You need a new female condom each time you have sex.

How do I get it?
- You do not need a prescription.
- You can buy it over-the-counter.

Possibility of getting pregnant
- (Number of pregnancies expected per 100 women who use this method for one year)
- Out of 100 women who use this method, about 20 may get pregnant.

Some Risks
- Irritation
- Allergic reactions

Does it protect me from sexually transmitted infections (STIs)?
- May give some protection against STIs.
- Not as effective as latex condoms.
- More research is needed.

Diaphragm with Spermicide

What is it?
- A dome-shaped flexible disk with a flexible rim.
- Made from latex rubber or silicone.
- It covers the cervix so that sperm cannot reach the egg.

How do I use it?
- You need to put spermicidal jelly on the inside of the diaphragm before putting it into the vagina.
- You must put the diaphragm into the vagina before having sex.
- You must leave the diaphragm in place at least 6 hours after having sex.
- It can be left in place for up to 24 hours. You need to use more spermicide every time you have sex.

How do I get it?
- You need a prescription.
- A doctor or nurse will need to do an exam to find the right size diaphragm for you.
- You should have the diaphragm checked after childbirth or if you lose more than 15 lbs., you might need a different size.

Possibility of getting pregnant
- (Number of pregnancies expected per 100 women who use this method for one year)
- Out of 100 women who use this method, about 15 may get pregnant.

Some Risks
- Irritation, allergic reactions, and urinary tract infection.
- If you keep it in place longer than 24 hours, there is a risk of toxic shock syndrome. Toxic shock is a rare but serious infection.

Does it protect me from sexually transmitted infections (STIs)
No.

Sponge with Spermicide

What is it?
A disk-shaped polyurethane device with the spermicide nonoxynol-9.

How do I use it?
- Put it into the vagina before you have sex.
- Protects for up to 24 hours. You do not need to use more spermicide each time you have sex.
- You must leave the sponge in place for at least 6 hours after having sex.
- You must take the sponge out within 30 hours after you put it in. Throw it away after you use it.

How do I get it?
- You do not need a prescription.
- You can buy it over-the-counter.

Possibility of getting pregnant
- (Number of pregnancies expected per 100 women who use this method for one year)
- Out of 100 women who use this method, 16-32 may get pregnant.
- It may not work as well for women who have given birth. Childbirth stretches the vagina and cervix and the sponge may not fit as well.

Some Risks
- Irritation and allergic reactions.
- Some women may have a hard time taking the sponge out.
- If you keep it in place longer than 24-30 hours, there is a risk of toxic shock syndrome. Toxic shock is a rare but serious infection.

Does it protect me from sexually transmitted infections (STIs)?
No.

Cervical Cap with Spermicide

What is it?
A soft latex or silicone cup with a round rim, which fits snugly around the cervix. It covers the cervix so that sperm cannot reach the egg.

How do I use it?
- You need to put spermicidal jelly inside the cap before you use it.
- You must put the cap in the vagina before you have sex.

- You may find it hard to put in.
- You must leave the cap in place for at least 6 hours after having sex.
- You may leave the cap in for up to 48 hours.
- You do NOT need to use more spermicide each time you have sex.

How do I get it?
- You need a prescription.

Possibility of getting pregnant
- (Number of pregnancies expected per 100 women who use this method for one year)
- Out of 100 women who use this method, about 17-23 may get pregnant.
- It may not work as well for women who have given birth. Childbirth stretches the vagina and cervix and the cap may not fit as well.

Some Risks
- Irritation, allergic reactions, and abnormal Pap test.
- If you keep it in place longer than 48 hours, there is a risk of toxic shock syndrome. Toxic shock is a rare but serious infection.

Does it protect me from sexually transmitted infections (STIs)?
No.

Spermicide Alone

What is it?
A foam, cream, jelly, film, or tablet that kills sperm.

How do I use it?
- Instructions can be different for each type of spermicide. Read the label before you use it.
- You need to put spermicide into the vagina between 5 and 90 minutes before you have sex.
- You usually need to leave it in place at least 6 to 8 hours after; do not douche or rinse the vagina for at least 6 hours after sex.

How do I get it?
- You do not need a prescription.
- You can buy it over-the-counter.

Possibility of getting pregnant
- (Number of pregnancies expected per 100 women who use this method for one year)
- Out of 100 women who use this method, about 30 may get pregnant.
- Different studies show different rates of effectiveness.

Some Risks
- Irritation.
- Allergic reactions
- Urinary tract infection.
- If you are also using a medicine for a vaginal yeast infection, the spermicide might not work as well.

Does it protect me from sexually transmitted infections (STIs)?
No.

Oral Contraceptives - The Pill

Combined Pill

Progestin-only

Extended/Continuous Use

Combined Pill

What is it?
- A pill that uses hormones (estrogen and progestin) to stop the ovaries from releasing eggs in most women.
- It also thickens the cervical mucus, which keeps the sperm from joining with the egg.

How do I use it?
You should swallow the pill at the same time every day, whether or not you have sex.

How do I get it?
- You need a prescription.

Possibility of getting pregnant
- (Number of pregnancies expected per 100 women who use this method for one year)
- Out of 100 women who use this method, about 5 may get pregnant.

Some Risks
- Dizziness.
- Nausea.
- Changes in your cycle (period).
- Changes in mood.
- Weight gain.

- It is not common, but some women who take the pill develop high blood pressure. It is rare, but some women will have blood clots, heart attacks, or strokes.

Does it protect me from sexually transmitted infections (STIs)?
No.

Progestin-only

What is it?
- A pill that has only the hormone progestin.
- It thickens the cervical mucus, which keeps the sperm from joining with the egg.
- Less often, it stops the ovaries from releasing eggs.

How do I use it?
You should swallow the pill at the same time every day, whether or not you have sex.

How do I get it?
- You need a prescription.

Possibility of getting pregnant
- (Number of pregnancies expected per 100 women who use this method for one year)
- Out of 100 women who use this method, about 5 may get pregnant.

Some Risks
- Irregular bleeding.
- Weight gain.
- Breast tenderness.
- Less protection against ectopic pregnancy (pregnancy in the fallopian tubes) than the combination pill.

Does it protect me from sexually transmitted infections (STIs)?
No.

Extended / Continuous Use

What is it?
- A pill that uses hormones (estrogen and progestin) to stop the ovaries from releasing eggs in most women.
- It also thickens the cervical mucus, which keeps the sperm from joining with the egg.
- These pills are designed so women have fewer or no periods.

How do I use it?
You should swallow the pill at the same time every day, whether or not you have sex.

How do I get it?
You need a prescription.

Possibility of getting pregnant
- (Number of pregnancies expected per 100 women who use this method for one year)
- Out of 100 women who use this method, about 5 may get pregnant.

Some Risks
- Risks are similar to other oral contraceptives.
- You may have fewer planned periods. If you miss a scheduled period, you may be pregnant.
- You will likely have more bleeding and spotting between periods than with other oral contraceptives.

Does it protect me from sexually transmitted infections (STIs)?
No.

Patch

What is it?
- This is a skin patch you can wear on the lower abdomen, buttocks, or upper body.
- It uses hormones (estrogen and progestin) to stop the ovaries from releasing eggs in most women.
- It also thickens the cervical mucus, which keeps the sperm from joining with the egg.

How do I use it?
- You put on a new patch and take off the old patch once a week for 3 weeks.
- During the fourth week, you do not wear a patch and you have a menstrual period.

How do I get it?
You need a prescription.

Possibility of getting pregnant
- (Number of pregnancies expected per 100 women who use this method for one year)
- Out of 100 women who use this method, about 5 may get pregnant.
- The patch may be less effective for women who weigh more than 198 lbs.

Some Risks

- It will expose you to higher than average levels of estrogen than most oral contraceptives.
- It is not known if serious risks, such as blood clots, are greater with the skin patch because of the greater exposure to estrogen.

Does it protect me from sexually transmitted infections (STIs)?
No.

Shot / Injection

What is it?

- A shot of the hormone progestin that stops the ovaries from releasing eggs in most women.
- It also thickens the cervical mucus, which keeps the sperm from joining with the egg.

How do I use it?
You need one shot every 3 months.

How do I get it?
You need a prescription.

Possibility of getting pregnant

- (Number of pregnancies expected per 100 women who use this method for one year)
- Out of 100 women who use this method, less than 1 may get pregnant.

Some Risks

- You may have bone loss if you get the shot for more than 2 years.
- Bleeding between periods.
- Weight gain.
- Breast tenderness.
- Headaches.

Does it protect me from sexually transmitted infections (STIs)?
No.

Emergency Contraception
May be used if you do not use birth control or if your regular birth control fails. It should not be used as a regular form of birth control.

"The Morning After Pill"

What is it?
- These are pills with hormones (either progestin alone or progestin plus estrogen) that are similar to other oral contraceptives.
- They stop the ovaries from releasing an egg or stops sperm from joining with the egg.

How do I use it?
- You can use these after you have unprotected sex (did not use birth control).
- You can also use these if your birth control did not work (i.e. the condom broke).
- You must swallow the pills within 72 hours of having unprotected sex.
- For the best chance for it to work, you should start taking the pills as soon as possible after unprotected sex.

How do I get it?
- You can buy it over the counter if you are 18 years or older.
- If you are younger than 18, you need a prescription.

Possibility of getting pregnant
- (Number of pregnancies expected per 100 women who use this method for one year)
- This method reduces the risk of pregnancy resulting from a single act of unprotected sex by almost 85 percent, if you take it within 72 hours.

Some Risks
Nausea, vomiting, abdominal pain, fatigue, and headache.

Does it protect me from sexually transmitted infections (STIs)?
No.

Implanted Devices
Are inserted into the body and can be kept in place for a few years.

IUD

What is it?
A T-shaped device that is put into the uterus by a health care provider.

How do I use it?
After a doctor or other health care provider puts in the IUD, it can stay in place for 5 to 10 years, depending on the type.

How do I get it?
- You need a prescription.

Possibility of getting pregnant
- (Number of pregnancies expected per 100 women who use this method for one year)
- Out of 100 women who use this method, less than 1 may get pregnant.

Some Risks
- Cramps
- Bleeding
- Pelvic inflammatory disease
- Infertility
- Tear or hole in the uterus

Does it protect me from sexually transmitted infections (STIs)?
No.

Implantable Rod

What is it?
- A thin, matchstick-sized rod that contains the hormone progestin.
- It thickens the cervical mucus, which keeps sperm from joining with the egg.
- Less often, it stops the ovaries from releasing eggs.

How do I use it?
- It is put under the skin on the inside of your upper arm.
- It lasts up to 3 years.

How do I get it?
A doctor or nurse needs to put it under the skin of your arm.
- You will get a shot in the upper arm to make the skin numb, then the rod is placed just under the skin with a needle.

Possibility of getting pregnant
- (Number of pregnancies expected per 100 women who use this method for one year)
- Out of 100 women who use this method, less than 1 may get pregnant.
- It might not work as well for overweight or obese women.
- It might not work as well if you are taking certain medicines for things like: tuberculosis (TB), seizures, depression, or HIV/AIDS.
- Tell your doctor if you are taking the herb St. John's Wort.

Some Risks
Acne, weight gain, cysts of the ovaries, mood changes, depression, hair loss, headache, upset stomach, dizziness, lower interest in sexual activity, sore breasts, and changes in your periods

Does it protect me from sexually transmitted infections (STIs)?
No.

Sterilization Surgery for Women

Trans-abdominal Surgical Sterilization / Surgical Implant

What is it?
- A device is placed on the outside of each fallopian tube. The woman's fallopian tubes are blocked so the egg and sperm can't meet in the fallopian tube. This stops you from getting pregnant.

How do I use it?
- This is a surgery a woman has only once.
- It is permanent.

How do I get it?
This is a surgery you ask for. You will need a small incision (cut) below the belly button and 2 or more smaller incisions (cuts).

Possibility of getting pregnant
- (Number of pregnancies expected per 100 women who use this method for one year)
- Out of 100 women who use this method, less than 1 may get pregnant.

Some Risks
- Pain
- Bleeding
- Infection or other complications after surgery
- Ectopic (tubal) pregnancy

Does it protect me from sexually transmitted infections (STIs)?
No.

Sterilization Implant for Women

Transcervical Surgical Sterilization Implant

What is it?
- Small flexible, metal coil that is put into the fallopian tubes through the vagina.
- The device works by causing scar tissue to form around the coil. This blocks the fallopian tubes and stops you from getting pregnant.

How do I use it?
- The device is put inside the fallopian tube with a special catheter.

- You need to use another birth control method during the first 3 months. You will need an X-ray to make sure the device is in the right place.
- It is permanent.

How do I get it?
- The devices are placed into the tubes using a camera placed in the uterus.
- Once the tubes are found, the devices are inserted. No skin cutting (incision) is needed.
- You may need local anesthesia.
- Since it is inserted through the vagina, you do not need an incision (cutting).

Possibility of getting pregnant
Out of 100 women who use this method, less than 1 may get pregnant.

Some Risks
- Mild to moderate pain after insertion
- Ectopic (tubal) pregnancy

Does it protect me from sexually transmitted infections (STIs)?
No.

nine

The Risks
The STDs of Sex

Mommies, I know this is a lot of information to soak up, but before you make a decision to become sexually active again you need to know all of the facts, choices, risks and complexities associated with that decision.

STDs are infections that are passed from person to person during sexual activity (vaginal, oral, or anal intercourse). **The only effective means to avoid becoming infected with or transmitting a sexually transmitted infection is to abstain from sexual intercourse (i.e., oral, vaginal, or anal sex).**

Some would conclude that having sexual intercourse only within a long-term, mutually monogamous relationship with an uninfected partner is an effective means to avoid becoming infected. That is misleading at best. Marriage is the only legitimate grounds for sex, and the only institution with a built in covenant of fidelity. A long-term, mutually monogamous relationship with an uninfected partner is as binding as a head nod or handshake.

Male latex condoms is the suggested route in reducing the transmission of HIV and other sexually transmitted infections, including gonorrhea, chlamydial infection and trichomoniasis, but again I pose the question, *"What happens if the condom breaks?"*

STD's: The Basics

What is an STD?

STD stands for *"sexually transmitted disease."* STDs are infections that are passed from person to person during sexual activity (vaginal, oral, or anal intercourse). Some STDs are curable, while others are not. It is estimated that more than 19 million new cases of STDs occur in the U.S. every year. Millions of these new cases occur among teenagers.

Who can get an STD?
Anyone who engages in intimate sexual contact can get an STD.

How do I know if I have an STD?

Since many STDs do not have any obvious symptoms, the only sure way to know if someone has an infection is by having a medical exam or a lab test. It is important to know that someone can get infected with an STD and not realize it for period of time. That is a risky time since an infected person can unknowingly pass the STD on to a partner. Getting tested is key to stopping the spread of infection.

Do latex condoms protect me from getting an STD?

Latex condoms significantly reduce your risk of getting most STDs, including HIV (the virus that causes AIDS), if you use them correctly every time. But latex condoms don't eliminate risk completely. Both male and female plastic condoms (made from polyurethane) provide some protection, but not as much as latex condoms. Though condoms can help protect you, research shows that they do not provide full protection against some STDs, such as human papillomavirus (HPV). Also, it's important for you to know that "skin" condoms (made from animal membrane) don't protect you at all.

Who can I talk to if I think I have an STD or want to learn more about prevention?

It is important to talk to your doctor to help diagnose you and to discuss treatment options.

What can happen if I get an STD?

Each STD has its own set of symptoms. However, many STDs can lead to similar long-term consequences, particularly if the STD goes untreated.

Pelvic inflammatory disease (PID) can damage fallopian tubes and make it difficult or impossible to have a baby, a problem called "infertility."

Chronic pain in the lower abdomen.

Tubal pregnancy, also called ectopic pregnancy, a condition in which the pregnancy grows in the fallopian tube instead of in the uterus. This problem is dangerous and requires immediate medical care.

Infection with some types of HPV has been linked to cancer of the cervix.

Males and females who are infected with STDs can transmit the infection to their partners. If pregnant, women can then transmit the infection to their babies.

If a person is infected with an STD they have a greater chance of contracting another STD.

STDs caused by bacteria (like chlamydia, gonorrhea, and syphilis) can usually be cured with antibiotics. If they are not treated early, serious long-term problems can develop, like pain, infertility, and even death.

What are some symptoms of common STDs?

Bacterial Vaginosis

Some women with BV don't know they have it because they have no symptoms.

Women who have never had sexual intercourse may also be affected by BV, and it is common in pregnant women.

Having BV can increase a woman's susceptibility to other STDs. Pregnant women may deliver premature or low birth-weight babies.

Although BV will sometimes clear up without treatment, all women with symptoms of BV should be treated to avoid complications. Male partners generally do not need to be treated. However, BV may spread between female sex partners.

Treatment is especially important for pregnant women. All pregnant women who have ever had a premature delivery or low birth weight baby should be considered for a BV examination, regardless of symptoms, and should be treated if they have BV. All pregnant women who have symptoms of BV should be checked and treated.

Some physicians recommend that all women undergoing a hysterectomy or abortion be treated for BV prior to the procedure, regardless of symptoms, to reduce their risk of developing an infection.

BV is treatable with antibiotics prescribed by a health care provider. Two different antibiotics are recommended as treatment for BV: metronidazole or clindamycin. Either can be used with non-pregnant or pregnant women, but the recommended dosages differ. Women with BV who are HIV-positive should receive the same treatment as those who are HIV-negative.

BV can recur after treatment.

Chlamydia

Chlamydia is the most commonly reported STD in the United States.

Sexually active females 25 years old and younger need testing every year.

Easy to cure, chlamydia can impact a woman's ability to have children if left untreated.

- 3/4 of infected females and 1/2 of infected males have no symptoms.

- Discharge from the genital organs.

- Burning with urination.

In females, lower abdominal and/or back pain and pain during intercourse.

Chlamydia can be easily treated and cured with antibiotics. A single dose of azithromycin or a week of doxycycline (twice daily) are the most commonly used treatments. HIV-positive persons with chlamydia should receive the same treatment as those who are HIV negative.

All sex partners should be evaluated, tested, and treated. Persons with chlamydia should abstain from sexual intercourse until they and their sex partners have completed treatment, otherwise re-infection is possible.

Women whose sex partners have not been appropriately treated are at high risk for re-infection. Having multiple infections increases a woman's risk of serious reproductive health complications, including infertility. Retesting should be encouraged three months after treatment of an initial infection. This is especially true if a woman does not know if her sex partner received treatment.

Gonorrhea

If they occur, symptoms in men and women vary depending on what part of the body is infected: Gonorrhea can affect the anus, eyes, mouth, genitals, or throat.

This disease can impact a woman's ability to have children if left untreated.

- Discharge from the genital organs.

- Burning or itching during urination.

- Pelvic pain.

- Females frequently have no symptoms.

Gonorrhea, one of the most common sexually transmitted diseases in the United States, has few treatment options. In April of last year, CDC updated its recommendations for gonorrhea treatment, no longer recommending fluoroquinolone antibiotics (ciprofloxacin, ofloxacin and levofloxacin), based on data indicating widespread drug resistance in the United States. As a result, the only CDC-recommended options for treating gonorrhea are in a single class of antibiotics known as cephalosporins. Within this class, the only recommended drug treatment for all types of gonorrhea (urogenital, rectal and pharyngeal) is an injection form, ceftriaxone. However, for uncomplicated gonorrhea (gonorrhea that has not spread to the blood or central nervous system) of the cervix, urethra or rectum, CDC also recommends an alternative to ceftriaxone – an oral treatment option, cefixime. Since 2002 that drug has been available only as a suspension (liquid form), which limited its utility, since a suspension is not as convenient as a tablet.

Syphilis

Syphilis is easy to cure in its early stages.

Signs and symptoms of syphilis include a firm, round, small, and painless sore on the genitals, anus, or mouth, or a rash on the body, especially on the palms of the hands or the soles of the feet.

In 2008, 63% of the reported primary and secondary (P&S) syphilis cases were among men who have sex with men (MSM).

During 2004–2008, rates of P&S syphilis increased the most among 15–24 year-old men and women.

- Painless sores on genitals (10 days to 3 months after infection).

- Rash (3 to 6 weeks after sores appear).

Syphilis is easy to cure in its early stages. A single intramuscular injection of penicillin, an antibiotic, will cure a person who has had syphilis for less than a year. Additional doses are needed to treat someone who has had syphilis for longer than a year. For people who are allergic to penicillin, other antibiotics are available to treat syphilis. There are no home remedies or over-the-counter drugs that will cure syphilis. Treatment will kill the syphilis bacterium and prevent further damage, but it will not repair damage already done.

Because effective treatment is available, it is important that persons be screened for syphilis on an on-going basis if their sexual behaviors put them at risk for STDs.

Persons who receive syphilis treatment must abstain from sexual contact with new partners until the syphilis sores are completely healed. Persons with syphilis must notify their sex partners so that they also can be tested and receive treatment if necessary.

Pelvic Inflammatory Disease (PID)

PID occurs when certain bacteria, such as chlamydia or gonorrhea, move upward from a woman's vagina or cervix (opening to the uterus) into her reproductive organs.

Women can protect themselves from PID by taking action to prevent STDs or by getting early treatment if they have any genital symptoms such as vaginal discharge, burning during urination, abdominal or pelvic pain, pain during sexual intercourse, or bleeding between menstrual cycles.

Prompt and appropriate treatment of PID can help prevent complications, including permanent damage to female reproductive organs.

PID can be cured with several types of antibiotics. A health care provider will determine and prescribe the best therapy. However, antibiotic treatment does not reverse any damage that has already occurred to the reproductive organs. If a woman has pelvic pain and other symptoms of PID, it is critical that she seek care immediately. Prompt antibiotic treatment can prevent severe damage to reproductive organs. The longer a woman delays treatment for PID, the more likely she is to become infertile or to have a future ectopic pregnancy because of damage to the fallopian tubes. Hospitalization to treat PID may be recommended if the woman (1) is severely ill (e.g., nausea, vomiting, and high fever); (2) is pregnant; (3) does not respond to or cannot take oral medication and needs intravenous antibiotics; (4) has an abscess in the fallopian tube or ovary (tubo-ovarian abscess); or (5) needs to be monitored to be sure that her symptoms are not due to another condition that would require emergency surgery (e.g., appendicitis). If symptoms continue or if an abscess does not go away, surgery may be needed. Complications of PID, such as chronic pelvic pain and scarring are difficult to treat, but sometimes they improve with surgery.

Trichomoniasis

The infection often has no symptoms although women are more likely than men to get symptoms. You may notice an unusual genital discharge.

Without treatment, trichomoniasis can increase a person's risk of acquiring HIV.

Pregnant women with trichomoniasis can deliver premature, low birth weight babies.

Trichomoniasis can usually be cured with prescription drugs, either metronidazole or tinidazole, given by mouth in a single dose. The symptoms of trichomoniasis may disappear within a few weeks without treatment. However, even infected people who never had symptoms or whose symptoms have stopped can continue to infect or re-infect partners until they have been treated. Therefore, both partners should be treated at the same time to eliminate the parasite. Persons being treated for trichomoniasis should avoid sex until they and their sex partners complete treatment and have no symptoms. Metronidazole can be used by pregnant women. Having trichomoniasis once does not protect a person from getting it again. Following successful treatment, people can still be susceptible to re-infection.

Genital Herpes

Itching, burning, or pain in the genital area.

Blisters or sores (sores may heal but can reappear throughout your life).

You can get genital herpes even if your partner shows no signs of the infection.

If you have any symptoms (like a sore on your genitals, especially one that periodically recurs)

There is no cure for herpes, but treatment is available to reduce symptoms and decrease the risk of transmission to a partner.

HIV/AIDS

HIV stands for Human Immunodeficiency Virus. HIV is the virus that causes AIDS.

Every 9½ minutes (on average), someone in the United States is infected with HIV, the virus that causes AIDS.

In 2006, an estimated 56,300 people became infected with HIV.

More than 1 million people in the United States are living with HIV.

Of those 1 million people living with HIV, 1 out of 5 do not know they are infected. (People who have HIV but don't know it can unknowingly pass the virus to their partners.)

Despite new therapies, people with HIV still develop AIDS.

Over 1 million people in the United States have been diagnosed with AIDS.

More than 14,000 people with AIDS still die each year in the United States.

What is HIV?

HIV stands for Human Immunodeficiency Virus. HIV is the virus that causes AIDS.

HIV is a virus that attacks your immune system. The immune system has "T cells" that help protect your body from disease. A person with HIV does not have as many "T cells" as a healthy person. HIV makes it hard for your body to fight off sickness.

A person with HIV is called HIV positive (HIV+).

How do you get HIV?

You can get HIV by:

* Having sex with a person who is HIV + and not using a condom consistently and correctly

* Sharing needles or syringes ("drug works") with someone who has HIV

* Getting blood from a person who has HIV

You can't get HIV by:

- Being in the same room with someone who has HIV.

- Sharing a knife or fork, sheets, toilet seats, or phones with someone who has HIV

- Kissing a person with HIV

- Shaking hands with someone with HIV

- Getting bitten by a mosquito or other bug

What are the signs and symptoms of HIV?

You cannot tell who has HIV just by looking at them. Most people do not show any outward signs when they first get HIV.

A person can spread HIV even if he or she does not look sick.

An HIV test is the only way to know for sure if you or someone else has HIV.

It may take a few weeks or months for the HIV to show up on a test. This is called the "window period". This means that a person who was just infected may not test positive, even though they have the virus. During the *"window period"* a person can pass the virus to others. Always protect yourself from HIV.

How can you prevent HIV?

- Get tested and know your HIV status so that you do not spread the virus.

- Before engaging in sexual activity with a partner, know their HIV status too.

- Use latex condoms consistently and correctly each time you have sex.

- Do not share needles.

How do you get tested for HIV?

There are 3 main types of tests for HIV:

- Blood - a small amount of blood is taken.

- Oral - a cotton swab is put in your mouth for about 2-5 minutes.

- Urine - a small cup of urine is tested.

How can you get treated for HIV?

There is no cure for HIV.

There are medicines that you can take to help stop the virus from building up in your body, so that you can stay mostly healthy.

What should pregnant women know about HIV?

- When a woman is pregnant, she can pass HIV to her fetus through her blood.

- A pregnant woman can take medicine to lower the chance of giving her baby HIV.

- HIV can get into her breast milk. A woman can pass HIV to her baby during breast feeding.

What can you do if you are HIV+?

- See your doctor often.

- Take your medicine. Medicines must be taken regularly, or it will get harder to treat the virus with those medicines.

- Eat a healthy, balanced diet.

- Don't smoke or use illegal drugs.

- Get regular exercise.

Prevention

How can I prevent getting an STD?

Abstinence (not having intimate sexual contact, including vaginal, anal, or oral sex) is the best way to prevent getting an STD. Abstinence is the only 100% guaranteed protection and prevention from contracting deadly sexually transmitted diseases.

Reduced Risks

For sexually active people, you can reduce the risk of infection by having sex with only one partner after both of you have been tested for STDs.

Using a latex or plastic condom every time you have sex helps reduce the risks. Proper condom use is even more important for people who have sex with multiple partners. Latex condoms can help protect against HIV/AIDS and other STDs, but they don't provide perfect protection.

If I am taking birth control pills, can I still get an STD?

YES! Birth control pills only reduce your chances of getting pregnant and do not provide protection against STDs. People who take birth control pills or use hormonal injections, patches, implants, or rings to prevent pregnancy should also use latex condoms.

What should I do if I think I might have an STD?

If you think you have been exposed to an STD, you should go to a clinic or doctor as soon as possible to be tested and treated. Health departments, which diagnose and treat STDs, are located in almost every county and city. They provide confidential information and will help answer any questions you have about STDs. You can locate a Family Planning clinic here:

www.hhs.gov/opa/familyplanning/database/index.html.

Should I have a checkup?

If you are sexually active, you should visit a clinic or doctor to be screened for STDs. Teens and adults who have had sex with more than one person are at greater risk of getting an STD such as HIV/AIDS

All of these sexually transmitted diseases can be treated, but only a few can be cured.

However you know what would be 100% effective?

You said it, *"ABSTINENCE! Yeahhhhhhh!"*

Okay, I know it's over the top, but we can save ourselves so much on the back end, if we can embrace abstinence until marriage. It's my responsibility to present you with well informed options.

In closing...

You see mommies you are not alone. I've been where you are and I overcame the struggle and so will you. This is not the end of the world for you, so don't give up. Your *dream has only been altered not abandoned*. To prove it to you a few previous teen mommies have shared their stories with you, to confirm what I have already told you; **YOU WILL MAKE IT!!!!!!**

WORDS OF WISDOM

ten

Words of Wisdom
Teen Virgins

Joya Rankins

Little Miss Joya is a bubbly 15 year-old student. Joya, being the smart young lady she is, already has her after high school plans set and rolling. Her plans are to attend college and receive a degree in education.

While attending college she will work part time as a model to help remove some of the financial burden from her mom. After college, she plans to secure a great job in her field of study, get married and have three children.

Joya does not have a boyfriend and she is still a virgin. Yeah!!! She thinks abstinence is important because of the risks associated with having sex. She doesn't want anything in the way of her future plans, and definitely feels that becoming sexually active will do just that. Joya doesn't want to get pregnant and she is not open to taking any chances of getting an STD.

Joya's been approached by a fellow peer to have sex and her answer is short and to the point, *"NO, I don't want to."* Joya knows a few teen mommies her age, and her heart goes out to them, because their lives have been totally changed. Joya, however, has the benefit of a great support system – her mom, dad, and other relatives – who address the topics and implications of sex before marriage.

Joya is on the right road to success. She is a very bright young lady who knows what she wants and is not afraid to work hard and stand on principle. Her enthusiasm is very rich and I can see that she won't let anything or anyone stand in her way. You Go Joya!!!!!!

Dreams Altered BUT NOT *Abandoned*

Asjha Cooper

Asjha Cooper is a 17 year-old high school graduate who excitedly expressed her post high school plans. She is in pursuit of a degree in Broadcast Journalism and desires to study abroad in an English speaking country to gain a world view perspective on life. How awesome is that.

In the meantime, Miss Asjha, who is quite the little actress, continues to take classes to perfect her craft. She has previously starred in several mainstream networks shows.

Her ambitions after college is to find credible employment as a news anchor, investigative reporter, or talk show host. She understands that she may have to begin with an entry-level position and work her way up, but she is prepared for the challenge.

Asjha does not have a boyfriend and she is okay with that; she is in no hurry to give up her virginity. Her Christian beliefs and knowing that abstinence is the right thing to do; she will not rush or be pressured into having sex. She has been approached to have sex, and her answer was a clear, *"NO."* She knows the risks and doesn't want to put herself in compromised predicaments. I can't say that I blame her.

When Asjha sees teen moms she feels quite sad, and wonders why they didn't wait or just protect themselves. Asjha's family is proactive and their approach to precaution is to engage in discussions about sex, and let Ashja know that she is by no means ready for such a huge responsibility. Ashja puts all her passion into her future and becoming a phenomenal actress that she doesn't have the time or energy to focus on sex.

Asjha is definitely the girl everyone should be on the lookout for. I know in my heart that we will all see her on the big screen one day. Asjha, keep rocking it!!!!

Lyric Coby

Lyric Coby is a 15 year-old beauty with aspirations to become a pediatrician. Lyric is a very active student who is not only very athletic, but is also following in her older sister's footsteps as a dedicated cheerleader.

Lyric already has her life mapped out and is not afraid of the stumbling blocks that may lie ahead. She knows what college she will attend and is already preparing for the transition. Lyric would love to have children one day, but knows that today is not that day. Good going, Lyric.

Her desire is to finish school and settle into her career first. Lyric has a boyfriend, but will not let that interfere with her dreams of attending college and receiving a degree. She shares that she and her boyfriend hardly ever talk about sex, because they both agree that it isn't going to happen. Lyric values abstinence until marriage, because that's what her parents raised her to believe.

Living under the same roof with both of her parents, they keep a watchful eye on her and the friends she entertains. She knows her parents will never steer her wrong, so she prefers to take their word than to find out the hard way. Lyric is one of few teenage girls who have not experienced the intense pressure of having sex by some sweet talking teenage boy. Some would say that Lyric has it pretty easy. Easy or not; pressured or not, Lyric deserves major credit for standing on her decision.

Lyric has quite a few friends who are teenage moms. She really feels sad for these mommies because now at such a young age they are met with a ton of responsibility. They potentially miss out on all the fun things that teenagers enjoy; like sleeping in, prom, and parties. Lyric is definitely right about the responsibility, we all know it's a lot of work. To make sure she stays on the right path her parents always talk with her about sex and STD's. So Miss Lyric knows to be aware.

Keep your eye on the prize Lyric; you will be there before you know. Good Job!!!

Dreams Altered BUT NOT *Abandoned*

Rebecca Gerber

Rebecca Gerber — the 15 year-old, horseback riding sensation —hopes to one day grace our presence on the big screen. Rebecca possesses the skills of a well-trained and gifted actress and there is no doubt in my mind that she will make this happen. She is very attentive and when she sets her mind on something, it will come to pass.

After graduating high school, Rebecca plans to go straight to college. Since she is uncertain about her major, she will start out taking general study classes. Rebecca is still on the right path. Though she may not be 100% sure about her major, she isn't putting off college until she decides. It's all about forward movement.

Rebecca has a boyfriend of 7 months, and even though they sometimes talk about sex, they both agree that they are not ready. I happen to have firsthand knowledge in this case, because Rebecca is dating my first born son Erique. Erique does not want to do anything to ruin his relationship with Rebecca, so he's not pressuring her about anything.

Rebecca is proving that she can overcome peer pressure and this is one of the main reasons why she remains abstinent. She feels that she is in charge of her own future and no one will stand in the way of her goals and dreams. Anyone who pressures Rebecca about sex knows the outcome; she drops them like a bad habit. Good job!!

Rebecca knows a few teen mommies, and she wonders how they handle all the responsibilities and finances of taking care of a baby. To make sure Rebecca remains baby free, her parents and friends always talks to her about abstinence and premarital sex. You can tell that Rebecca is paying attention and taking it all in. She understands that getting pregnant is not the only consequence of having sex, but the real threat of STD's and the emotional stress that also comes with having sex. With such a strong support system around her, Rebecca has a great formula for success. I'm so proud of you Rebecca; I can see you at the Oscars!

Mariah Wright

Mariah Wright is a 14 year-old California dance fanatic. After high school she will be trading in her leotard for a stethoscope. Wow, medical school; what a fabulous career road to travel. Little Miss Mariah already knows what it will take to get her to her final destination; no boys, good grades, and determination. I'd say that she is well on her way considering her goal to remain a virgin until she is married.

Mariah has even decided not to have a boyfriend because she wants to remain a virgin. No one has ever pressured Mariah to have sex, but if they did she would definitely tell them to hit the road. Mariah knows a few teen moms, and she knows their lives have changed drastically. Her heart goes out to these young mommies, because of the great level of responsibility that goes into taking care of themselves and their babies. Their missing out on "teen-hood" really breaks her heart.

To help Mariah stay on the right path, she has candid conversations regarding sex before marriage and the importance of abstinence with her family, teachers, and counselor. They truly want to see her succeed, and contribute by being the support system she needs.

Mariah is well aware of the other risks associated with having sex outside of getting pregnant. She is educated about STD's and the emotional break downs and neither are worth jeopardizing her future, her body or her life.

Kudos to you, Mariah. I'm very proud of you and I can't wait to call you Dr. Wright. I know you will get there, just keep the faith.

Kinshara Burkes

Kinshara is a 37 year-old Product Development Manager for a major retailer in Texas. Kinshara became a teen mom at the age of 18 while attending college. Though some may argue that Kinshara, at 18, was considered an adult, the reality is that she was still a child.

She dated her 25 year-old boyfriend for a little more than a year before she became pregnant. Needless to say, she thought once she told him about the pregnancy, he would undoubtedly be very supportive and understanding. Wrong. Kinshara was forced to tell her parents about her pregnancy on her own. Aside from already feeling afraid and wondering, *"Oh my, what do I do now,"* Kinshara shared that she was most afraid of her parents.

To Kinshara's surprise her parents reactions were very different than she expected. Her mom was nurturing and assured her that everything was going to be okay, that she could do this, and extended an invitation to come back home. Her father's reaction was supportive as well; he just confirmed that they would get through it.

To support her baby, Kinshara worked a part-time job, applied for government assistance, and received financial assistance from her very supportive family. The baby's father remained **absent the entire time.** Before the pregnancy, Kinshara viewed school as secondary; having realized that she would become a mother at an early age; it motivated her to make school more of a priority.

Kinshara received a bachelor's degree in Fashion Merchandising. She wanted to set an example for her baby and provide for all her needs, and felt that her college degree would be the first step. She knew she had to mature quickly and get it together, because she refused to be part of the government aid assistance forever.

I asked Kinshara had anyone every talked to her about premarital sex and the topic of safe sex, and she said, *"No."*

Kinshara's daughter in now a teenager and Kinshara consistently talks to her about sex from the avenues of safe sex, premarital and abstinence. Kinshara even went so far as to purchase her daughter a true love waits ring, and we all know that true love will wait.

When Kinshara sees other teen mom or pregnant teens, it takes her back to the moment when she found out she was pregnant. She passes no judgment on these young ladies, but thinks to herself, *"If they only knew,"* and for those who keep repeating the act, she asks herself, *"Why?"* If Kinshara had the opportunity to talk to teen girls who feel they are ready for sex, she would tell them, *"It's not what you think."* She would also tell them, *"Sex brings on more than just sex, it's not just physical, it's emotional. Sexual relations often create false emotions that confuse the entire situation."*

Though Kinshara loves her daughter to pieces, she shared that if she could go back in time she would have waited to have sex and waited for marriage to have her daughter.

Kinshara's relationship with her daughter puts a smile on my face. They are so close and Kinshara is raising and teaching her the right way. You can also tell that Kinshara doesn't have regrets because her daughter is worth it.

"Great job Kinshara, you are an awesome mommy!"

Dreams Altered BUT NOT Abandoned

Moniqua Rufus

Moniqua is a 24 year-old married mother of 3 and expecting another. She is employed as a Correctional Officer at a South Texas prison. Moniqua became pregnant at the age of 14 and a teen mommy at 15. She dated her boyfriend for 6 months before she became pregnant. When she told him about his upcoming fatherhood, Moniqua immediately felt his lack of support, and was faced with telling her mother on her own. "Wow, doesn't this sound familiar?"

Moniqua's mother was very disappointed. She had such high hopes for her daughter and wanted so much more for her. Moniqua's father passed away a few years before so he was not a part of this event.

Moniqua relied solely upon her mother for financial support to provide for herself and her baby. Well, that is until Moniqua came in contact with a very special and caring parenting teacher, Mrs. Brooks. With her guidance and encouragement, at 16, Moniqua secured employment at Subway and took some of the financial burden off of her mom.

In spite of the many adversities, Moniqua found the strength to finish high school, go on to college, and eventually received her degree in Criminal Justice. Moniqua knew that in order to be successful and provide a good life for her baby, she had to finish college. She was always a good student and made good grades and she was without excuse. She had the encouragement of her 3 sisters along with her mom who willingly took care of her baby while she went to school.

Moniqua mentioned that no one really talked to her about sex: premarital sex, safe sex, abstinence or otherwise, to the extent that was needed. But, as soon as everyone found out she was pregnant, they all had something to say. Even though Moniqua doesn't have any girls she made a commitment to definitely talk to her boys about sex and all its consequences.

Moniqua sees a lot of teenage girls who are now mommies; yet in spite of their immaturity, they keep having more and more babies. This breaks her heart. She adamantly talks to her young nieces about her struggle; about how hard it was to balance work, school, and baby; how she felt she wasn't able to be a child, because she had to take care of one. Moniqua hopes that her nieces take heed and think about all the consequences of sex.

Her advice for all teen mommies is to have faith and trust that you will make it. You are not alone and if possible, lean on family. Although Moniqua wasn't able to attend college parties, have an extended viewette career, or travel extensively, she is very grateful for her baby boy.

If she could turn back time, she would slap her young self for being so naïve.

In spite of it all, Moniqua is a very good mother, wife, and employee. These young ladies can learn a lot from Mrs. Moniqua.

"Kudos to you!"

Tequilla Cooper

Two words: Tequilla Cooper – a 33 year-old motivational lyricist – who became a teen mommy at the age of 16. Her pregnancy discovery was not the result of an at-home pregnancy test, but by way of the changes in her young body. Besides, she was in such denial, that she avoided taking the test for 3 months. Once her pregnancy was confirmed she felt a numbing sensation. She was afraid primarily because of the instability and dysfunction in her home, but was also a little excited at the same time.

She dated her 16 year-old boyfriend for a year before she became pregnant. Unlike so many of the previous stories, Tequilla's boyfriend was very caring and supportive. He was also afraid, but never turned his back on the little Cooper girl from the Windy City. "How awesome is that?"

Here is where Tequilla's story differed; her mother wanted her to have an abortion. "Wow." Since she lived under her mother's roof, Cooper thought she had to do as her mother instructed. But with a run of interference and a twist of fate; Cooper was too far along to have an abortion and had to continue with her pregnancy. Tequilla, was happy about the outcome of the pregnancy, but immediately subjected to intense cruelty from her mother, the one person whose love and support could have made a difference.

Her mother proceeded to tell her that no one would ever want her and that she succeeded at ruining her life. The cruelty Tequilla endured probably felt like it lasted a life time, but it was short-lived because Tequilla's mother kicked her and the baby out of the house for no apparent reason.

Tequilla was then forced to live in a two-bedroom apartment with her drug addicted father, step-mother and four children. After she lived in those cramped quarters for a year, which probably seemed more like an eternity, Tequilla and the father of her precious little girl decided that it was best for them to all be under one roof.

Tequilla never filed for government assistance, so she and the father had to work full-time jobs. Neither of them had any issues with working, because they both wanted to provide for their baby girl.

Tequilla dropped out of school in her senior year and obtained her GED. This eliminated work schedule conflicts and allotted more time for her to dedicate to her daughter which met her utter determination to be a great mommy. Cooper and the baby's father married and were together for the next 14 years.

Tequilla overcame her struggles because she understood that her life was not over and she just kept going. She wore multiple hats and took it all in stride. She was mommy, wife, provider, and a musical sensation who gained the opportunity to travel around the world and express her art through rap.

Tequilla received the watered down version of conversations regarding sex. She was taught that if don't have sex, you don't get pregnant, because if you do the man will leave you. Tequilla's daughter is now a teenager, and they have open conversations regarding sex. She's even taken her daughter to the doctor for consultative discussions about STD's. Tequilla wants to make sure her daughter does not follow in her footsteps; and even though she and her daughter's father are no longer together, he and his family continues to play a very active role in their daughter's life.

When Tequilla sees new teen mommies, she says to herself, "Oh my, that was me," and wonders if that was how she looked when she was a little girl with a baby on the way. Tequilla asks the question, "Why," when a teenage girl thinks she is ready to have sex. Tequilla knows in her heart that they are not ready for the consequences that follow.

The advice that Tequilla shares with all teen mommies is, "Your life is not over. Please remain in school and plan for your future. This will pass." Looking back Tequilla was a little saddened that she wasn't able to attend her prom and at 16 she felt as though someone pressed the button on a time machine and she suddenly turned 21. She wanted to go to college and become a teacher. Sometimes she wondered who Tequilla was outside of being a mother, but not once did she have any regrets about her daughter.

Tequilla's story touched my heart in a special way. I even teared up a couple times during our conversation. There were many obstacles in her path, but she kept fighting through to become a good mom and break that cruel cycle at the same time.

"Tequilla you are one mother who has so much heart and I am so proud of you. Hold your head up high; you are not what they said you are. You've proven to be so much more!"

Dreams Altered BUT NOT *Abandoned*

Ana Reyes

Ana Reyes is a feisty 39 year-old east coast native and mother of two. Though she possesses great strength and a take charge attitude, she knows what it feels like to be afraid and unsure.

Ana found out she was pregnant at the age of seventeen and was afraid that her mother was going to kill her. She didn't know what would happen or what to do. She actually waited until she was three months pregnant before she finally told her mother; and the expected outcome was the outcome. Her mother was very upset, but could do nothing because Ana was already pregnant.

Ana dated her child's father for three years before she became pregnant. In the beginning, he was very excited and quite supportive. Four years later, baby number two came along; and with the addition of another child came the subtraction of the support from the father. When the diminished support transitioned into no support at all, he forced Ana's hand and she filed for child support. Ana did what any good mother would do to make ends meet – she worked – two jobs no less. She was not going to let her babies go without.

Even more amazing was that while she worked two jobs, she also enrolled in school and continued her education. School was always important to Ana; so dropping out of high school was not an option. She attended school right up until the day she delivered her little bundle of joy and it was well worth it.

Post delivery and post high school, Ana received a certificate in Travel and Tourism, and was well on her way to financial security. Her struggle proved positive; she overcame, pushed forward, stayed in school, and focused on her children.

When Ana was young, her parents always talked to her about sex, from abstinence to safe sex. Ana like most teenage girls, thought she knew everything and that it wouldn't happen to her.

Ana always talks with her kids about sex and its consequences with the hope that they will not follow in her footsteps. She encourages them to finish school, establish a career, and then they can think about the opposite sex. She really wants them to avoid the struggles she endured and achieve more.

When Ana sees other teen mommies, she feels badly for them. She sympathizes with the struggle, and wishes she could help each and every one of them. She also encourages them not give up; and not abandon their dreams.

To all the teenagers who feel that they are ready for sex Ana tells them, "No, please don't do it. You are not ready. There are too many risks and the risks are not worth it."

If she could go back, she wouldn't change a thing; she adores her kids, and won't trade them for all the money in the world.

"Ana, I congratulate you for being such an amazing mother. Your children are so fortunate to have you as their mom. You went through the struggle and beat it hands down. I applaud you!"

Dreams Altered BUT NOT *Abandoned*

Stacy Sanders

Stacy Sanders – a beautiful 26 year-old southern belle from the great state of Texas – is currently the Social Media/Digital Brand Marketing Associate for a very prominent East Texas company.

At the age of nineteen, Stacy found out that she was expecting a baby. Although reality hadn't officially kicked in, she still experienced an initial shock. Stacy dated the father of her baby for two years and had no problem telling him that she was pregnant.

In the beginning, he was very supportive and said that he would do what he needed to do as a father.

Now Stacy was reluctant to tell her parents about the pregnancy. She normally assumed that her mother would be nurturing and her father would be angry and blow up. Quite the contrary, her mother was quite emotional and expressed her disappointment. She even broached the subject of abortion, but in her heart could not continue down that road. Stacy's father was the consoling parent. He let her know that everything would be alright and they would get past it.

Stacy lived with her mother and continued to go to college. In order to provide for her baby, she worked fulltime and accepted as much overtime as possible. By this time, her baby's father was not as supportive. When she became financially stable and no longer needed to ask for assistance, she and her baby moved into their own apartment. Not long after acquiring her independence, along came baby number two.

Stacy was still not deterred from her goal of finishing school. In fact it motivated her even more. She wanted her children to witness her perseverance; that she never gave up, so dropping out was not an option. What normally took four years, took Stacy eight, but she obtained a Bachelors degree in Marketing. *"That mommies; is called determination."* Stacy would have not been able to do it without the love and support of her family and children's godmother. Stacy held on to her faith in God, and knew that He would see her through.

Even though Stacy's mom was strict and talked with her about sex, she, like many teen girls, didn't think it would happen to her. With all Stacy has gone through, she understands the importance of talking to her children about sex. Her daughters are not quite ready for that talk just yet, but rest assured it's on the agenda.

For young girls who feel they are ready for sex, Stacy's advice is to hold off. She doesn't want them to look back with regrets. She would also like to encourage teen mommies to stay positive and don't give up. *"Please try and give your baby the best life possible; not necessarily money and physical things, but inspiration and support."*

If Stacy could turn back time, the only thing she would change is the baby's father. "Does this sound familiar?" She loves both of her girls and wouldn't give them up for the world.

"Stacy I'm so proud of you. Your determination is fascinating and I applaud you for not letting anything or anyone stand in your way. You are a great mommy!"

Dreams Altered BUT NOT *Abandoned*

Jessica Chester

Jessica Chester is a 24 year-old who works in the Family Planning Outreach department for a major hospital in Dallas, TX. Jessica had her first baby at seventeen and had her second at the age of eighteen.

When Jessica found out she was pregnant, the first thing that popped into her mind was that she had disappointed her mother. After telling her mom, she waited for the disappointment speech, but instead her mother wrapped her arms around her and reassured her that everything would be alright.

Equally supportive was the father of the baby. They dated a little over year before she became pregnant. When she informed him about the baby, somehow he already knew. Maybe he had a gut feeling, who knows. He showed his support while she was pregnant, and rubbed her tummy, gave her foot massages, and lots of hugs, and kisses. Wow!

Jessica received assistance from her mom and the baby's father, who became her husband. Jessica was a fulltime student, who graduated at the top 1% of her high school class. She was awarded a full scholarship from a major Dallas university. So, instead of working, she applied for and used student loans to help her husband pay bills, and afford daycare. "You go Jessica!"

While in college, she rarely missed a day, she even took the kids to school with her so that she didn't miss an event. Jessica was involved in the Christians on Campus Organization, Black Students Alliance, Power Dance, and President of her Alpha Kappa Alpha Sorority chapter.

It still doesn't end there. Jessica graduated pre-med with a 4.5 gpa and a double degree in Molecular Biology and Business Administration. She is currently studying for the MCAT so she can enter medical school. "Dang! This lady is super smart." Jessica knew from the start that school was not optional. And for everyone who said she wouldn't make it… Boom, in your face! Jessica accomplished all of this with the support from her mother, baby's father, and family friends who volunteered as babysitters when she needed relief from all the pressure.

No one really talked to Jessica about sex, so to make sure history doesn't repeat itself; Jessica has already initiated conversations with her children about the parts of their bodies and their proper names. Once they get a little older she will have the birds and the bees talk.

As part of the family planning outreach, Jessica is responsible for speaking to teenage girls about sex, protection, and STD's. In these meetings a lot of the girls become nervous or embarrassed with the open dialogue. Jessica tells them, *"If you can't say the words then you're not ready to what they represent."* Jessica really enjoys her work, because it allows her to give back.

Looking back over her life, Jessica has no regrets, and is extremely grateful for her family.

"Jessica, you are a force to be reckoned with. Your story is absolutely phenomenal. You have accomplished so much in such a short time, with so many odds against you. You are indeed a role model. You have now given so many young mommies so much hope. I am completely in awe. You have a great journey ahead of you and I can't wait to address you as Dr. Jessica Chester, MD. You go girl!"

Dreams Altered BUT NOT *Abandoned*

Alice Burkholder

Meet Alice Burkholder, a sweet 40 year-old mother from Southern California. This mild-mannered mommy became pregnant at the age of seventeen. She dated the father of her baby for 4 years, who was also a teenager. She was in a state of shock and had no idea what to do next or how she was going to make it through this.

With great apprehension, she proceeded to tell her parents, and she knew how they would respond. As she anticipated, they were quite upset. Besides, no parent wanted to hear that their teenage daughter was pregnant. But they all knew that together they would get past that moment.

The father of Alice's baby was not all that supportive, which caused her to rely solely on her parents until she graduated high school. Dropping out was not an option for Alice and her parents reinforced that ideal. After graduation, she worked two jobs as a means to provide for her and her baby. Because Alice understood the value of education, she enrolled in evening classes to obtain her Banking and Finance Certification. She was so determined that she took the baby to school with her when she couldn't find a babysitter.

Alice's hard work set a great example for her child and became a testament of her fortitude; she never gave up. She was now responsible for the life of another and overcame her struggles. With support and understanding from her family, she knew she would succeed.

Alice and her family never really held discussions about sex when she was a child, but she was aware of the consequences. She went to the doctor to get birth control pills, but even the pill could not prevent pregnancy. They only guaranteed 99% and Alice conceived while she was on the pill.

"Mommies, I didn't say that to scare you. Well, actually that's a lie. I did tell you to scare you. You need to be made aware of all the facts before you make the decision to have sex, and aside from only being 99% effective, the pill won't protect you from STD's.

Okay, let's get back on track. ;-)"

Alice is very determined to make sure her children do not experience what she went through, so she always talks to them about sex, and how important it is to wait. She knows they are not ready for the emotional and tangible consequences involved and their focus is better directed toward school.

For the teen mommies, Alice wants you to get a plan, focus on school, and then aspire to be a mom. Alice may have missed out on her school prom and homecoming, but her baby was much more important than either one of those, and as a mommy, she did what she had to do.

"Alice, you are an awesome mom. There are a lot of mommies who can learn from you. It takes a real mom to choose to be with her baby, rather than solicit babysitter after babysitter to watch them while you go have fun. I give you two thumbs up!"

Dreams Altered BUT NOT Abandoned

Koreyan Crain

Koreyan Crain is a 34 year-old Registered Nurse from the great state of Texas. Koreyan became a mommy at 19 years of age. When she discovered she was pregnant, she thought her life had come to an end. Her thoughts immediately moved to having to abandon school in order to get a job. She even thought her mom would kick her out of the house. Needless to say, her mom was very upset; she even refrained from speaking to Koreyan for weeks. The silver lining was that her father was very excited and earnestly anticipated the arrival of his first grandchild.

Eventually Koreyan's mom came around but was still very disappointed. Koreyan was acquainted with the father of her baby for quite some time. They went to school together, but in spite of their history, he ultimately withdrew his support from her and the baby.

Koreyan's aunt was able to assist her with getting a job. She worked for a well-known dialysis center in East Texas. She made well above minimum wage and was very blessed with the means to financially support herself and her baby. The baby's father was not around and ended up serving time in and out of jail, which left the burden of responsibility on Koreyan.

While holding down her job and taking care of her baby, Koreyan realized she needed to return to school. Before her pregnancy, school was just semi-important to her, but after having the baby, it became more of a priority. She initially enrolled to become an LVN (Licensed Vocational Nurse), but that wasn't enough for her. Once her daughter was of school age, Koreyan went to school to become a Registered Nurse and received a Bachelor's Degree in Nursing.

Koreyan's road was tough, but she knew if she failed, it would negatively impact her daughter. She kept going and placed her trust in God. Her struggle continued when in 2008, she was diagnosed with cervical cancer and still did not become discouraged. She kept the faith and kept it moving. Koreyan's cancer has now been in remission for fourteen months. God showed up in an awesome way; He made a way out of no way.

No one in Koreyan's family discussed matters of sex. Most of what she learned, she picked up in school, but nothing on a personal level. In an effort not to emulate the mistakes of the past, Koreyan talks with her daughter regularly about sex. She wants her to learn the facts from her, not by way of rumor from friends in school. Koreyan even went a step further and gave her daughter a coming of age party when she started menstruating. Koreyan and other moms talked to the girls at the party about their bodies and engaged in topics on abstinence, and safe sex. She has gone the extra mile to ensure that her daughter is well informed.

Her advice to all teen mommies is, *"Never give up. Life is not over, but is a series of choices you make moving forward."*

"Koreyan, all I can say is, "Wow." I really admire how you were able to keep the faith even when your health was compromised. You are a great mom, and I know your daughter appreciates you so much. I'm really proud of you, and I can't wait to see what's next. Be blessed!"

Dreams Altered BUT NOT Abandoned

Erica Thompson

Erica Thompson, 29 year-old, mother of three who had her first baby at the age of 16. Erica was a very active teenager, and when she found out she was pregnant she was horrified. She was doing well in school, a part of the school's drill team and did not want to give that up. In a moment of panic, she contemplated abortion and thought it would be the best option. But she could not go through with it, and quickly regretted her selfish thoughts. Instead, she continued with the pregnancy and managed to keep it hidden for a whole six months.

Erica dated the father of her baby for nearly a year, and he was really excited about his upcoming fatherhood. Erica's mom, on the other hand was very upset. She knew what great potential her daughter possessed and didn't want anything to get in the way of that. Due to her mother's failing health, Erica lived with her older sister, but once she became pregnant, her mother invited her to come home as long as she went to school; and she did just that.

After graduation, Erica worked two jobs to support herself and the baby. She was employed at the local carwash and a neighborhood fast food restaurant. By now the initial support from the father had drastically declined. Once she was finally on her feet and able to make ends meet, Erica enrolled into a major university and completed 3 years of course study toward her Bachelors Degree. Erica always knew she would go to college, and did not let go of that dream. A degree provided Erica with more options to make a better life for her children. Erica's accomplishments can be partially attributed to the love and support she received from her family.

In Erica's home growing up, there was no talk about sex; it was not even open for discussion, so everything she learned came from her peers. Peers are great for social interaction, but more times than not may steer you in the wrong direction on life matters.

Erica made a vow to be more open with her children. She doesn't leave the tender subject of sex in the hands of their friends who have no clue themselves. At an early age she started teaching them about their body parts, and as they get older, she will broaden the subject.

Erica wants teenage girls to know that they have their whole lives ahead of them. There are too many incurable diseases to contend with; and it's just better to wait until marriage. She would also like to encourage them to hold their heads up; don't give up and please remain in school.

If Erica could go back in time she would graduate from college, get married, and then have her same three children. They are her world and she couldn't see life without them.

"Erica a.k.a Tasha, I'm very proud of you. I've seen your mothering skills with my own eyes and you deserve to be applauded. You are a fantastic mother, and are raising your children so well. They are respectable and impeccably presentable. A lot of mothers can learn from you; not just teen mommies; all mommies. You should be very proud of yourself and don't let anyone make you feel differently. Great job!"

Dreams Altered BUT NOT *Abandoned*

Lanacia Rachel

Mrs. Lanacia Rachel is a 34 year-old wife and mother of three who works as an administrative assistant at the corporate office of a major retailer in the North Texas area. Lanacia, like the rest of us was also a teen mom. When she discovered that she was pregnant at the age of seventeen, all she could say was, *"Oh my goodness."* She had no clue what to do. You see, Lanacia already made plans to attend Clark University in Atlanta, but with the new addition to the family, that was not possible and there was no support system in Atlanta.

Lanacia also feared her parent's reaction to the news. Instead of telling her mom first, she stayed with her father a few days while she developed the nerve to confront her mother. She was able to have her father accompany her when she shared her news. Lanacia's mother was very upset, because of the high hopes she had for her, but that didn't stop her from supporting her daughter and granddaughter.

In the beginning, the father-to-be was very supportive, until the baby was born. His mother was against the young couple's relationship which caused a great divide, so Lanacia was left alone to care for her baby.

After high school graduation, Lanacia found a job that required her to work 12 hour shifts, and rely on her parents to take care of the baby while she was at work. Lanacia still had not abandoned the idea of attending school. After her third child, she was ready to go back and enrolled in a Web Design and Media Production certificate program. Lanacia and her husband started their own media company with plans to expand greatly over the next few years. Lanacia felt that education was a key factor toward achieving that goal. Her determination was focused and fueled around her children and the example she wanted to set for them.

When Lanacia was a teenager, she and her family never talked about sex, so there was no real consciousness around the consequences. She promised not to make that same mistake with her children. She already explained to them that there are consequences that accompany sex, and that they are not ready for either; sex or the consequences.

To Lanacia, being a teen mommy is so common now. It's no longer considered to be taboo. If she could talk to teen girls, she would tell them to wait. There are so many things to experience that she doesn't want them to miss out on. Besides, with all the STD's, it's really not worth the risk. Lanacia shares with the teen mommies, *"It's going to be okay. There are a lot of programs to assist you, so don't quit and continue to pursue your dreams."*

Lanacia has no regrets and she is proud to be a mommy. She is such a determined mommy and has not given up on her dreams,. When she sets her mind to something she gets it done, and nothing stands in her way.

"Lanacia you are doing your thing, and I know God has big things in store for you. So keep up the good work, and continue to work towards you dream. Keep winning!"

Dreams Altered BUT NOT *Abandoned*

LaChander Crockett

Ms. LaChander Crockett is an outgoing, spontaneous 40 year-old mother of two. This flashy mommy spends her days employed in admitting at a hospital in the Oklahoma City area and her nights are spent living life to the fullest.

LaChander became pregnant when she was eighteen. Her story was a little different from ours. She was married a few months before she conceived. Although she married at a young age, she remained in school. When she found out she was pregnant, the first thing that came to mind was that she wanted to graduate on time. In order to accomplish her goal, LaChander enrolled into an alternative school, and knocked out her remaining school credits.

LaChander's parents were disappointed that she got pregnant so soon. Her mother even asked her why she hadn't taken birth control. At this point, there was nothing anyone could do. LaChander's husband was quite supportive; they were both still very young and just started their lives together. They knew it would not be easy. He worked fulltime to support the family, and both of their moms chipped in on their expenses; while LaChander attended school fulltime to obtain her college degree. After she received an Associates of Science Degree, she joined the workforce as well. LaChander was determined to make it and to prove to all naysayers wrong; and she did.

When LaChander was young, the only thing her family told her about sex was that it was bad. They never explained to her about getting pregnant or the different types of STD's. All she knew was that you weren't supposed to do it, she didn't know why; she just knew not to do it. That only sparked curiosity around the subject and we've all heard the saying, *"curiosity killed the cat."*

LaChander decided not to let history repeat itself. She made sure her daughters knew about sex, to avoid having to go through what she went through. Sometimes patterns of behavior are passed down through generations and LaChander put a halt to it.

Her advice to teen girls is, *"Be selfish. Be selfish enough to put your education first, and do all the things you want before you have children and have no regrets. Be selfish enough not to let anyone stand in the way of your career. You see, once you have kids you have to become selfless so that your children can one day have those same selfish opportunities."*

LaChander would also like to tell teen mommies to finish school so you can achieve your goals. *"Make the statistics out of a lie. You can make it, but need to protect yourself from getting pregnant again until you are married. It's hard to make it with one baby, but even harder with two."*

Looking back LaChander knows in her heart that she should not have married so young. She just wasn't ready to be a wife and mother. But, please don't misunderstand, her daughters are most important to her, and she wouldn't give them up for anything.

"LaChander, I'm so proud of you. You have such an awesome spirit, and I know your girls adore you for everything you sacrificed for them. Keep moving forward, because the best is yet to come. Love ya!"

Acknowledgements

First and foremost, I want to thank my Lord and Savior Jesus Christ, for all the blessings He has bestowed on me, even when I didn't deserve them.

My two precious sons; Erique and Uriah, *"I love you guys forever and a day."*

To my mother Catherine Sue Thomas, *"You are the best."*

King Hollis thanks for your encouragement and allowing me the time to write and do nothing else.

Mandy Teefey, *"Thank you so much for being a part of this creation, you know the struggle and have succeeded greatly."*

Alexia Allina, *"Thank you for all your PR help; I'm so grateful."*

Deneen Matthews, *"Thank you for all your help for this first time writer. I don't know what I would have done without you."*

Ed Harris, *"Thanks for taking time out of your busy schedule to take my "purdee" pictures, you rock."*

Sandra "Shelly" Cadena, *"Thank you so much for being a great friend. It was your faith that showed me how to be faithful."*

I thank the lovely teens who allowed me to interview them; Rebecca Gerber, Joya Rankins, Asjha Cooper, Mariah Wright and Lyric Coby.

I give a huge thank you and smooches to all my previous teen mommies who are putting it down and moving forward; Erica Thompson, Kinshara Burkes, Moniqua Rufus, Tequilla Cooper, Ana Reyes, Stacy Sanders, Jessica Chester, Alice Burkholder, Koreyan Crain, Lanacia Rachel, and LaChander Crockett.

I want to thank and give a great big hug to: my dad Sonny Mills, Larry Sanders, Brenda Champion, Ann Coby, Larry Mills, Dr. Sonny Acho, Linda Mills, Trenard Mills (My big bro), Didi Pace, Nikki Pace, Tony Coby (my big cuz/bro), Sara Miller, Amy Stewart, Chris Kuechenmeister, Aurora Gonzalez, Deanna McKinley, Bernie Gerber, Sugar Slade, Michelle Wright, Debra Mack (Queen), Pat Baptiste, Marcus Mack, Glenda Hines, Melanie Hines, Torin Wallace, Kenneth Thompson, Deshun Jackson, Donald Bishop, Calvin Williams, Arthur Gregg, Brian Kelley, Rodney Sherrard, Theo Wallace, George Moore, and Esmeralda Jones,.

Last but not least the U.S. Department of Health and Human Services, for providing a wealth of information and allowing me to share it.

References

http://www.acf.hhs.gov/programs/cb/stats_research/afcars/trends.htm

Burkman, et al., "Morbidity Risk Among Young Adolescents Undergoing Elective Abortion" Contraception, 30:99-105 (1984); "Post-Abortal Endometritis and Isolation of Chlamydia Trachomatis," Obstetrics and Gynecology 68(5):668- 690, (1986)

http://www.cdc.gov/std/default.htm

http://www.livestrong.com/article/165925-programs-to-help-teen-mothers/#ixzz12Mbvl1cv

www.hud.gov/offices/pih/other/sch/about.cfm

http://www.fns.usda.gov/wic/benefitsandservices/foodpkgregs.HTM

http://nccic.acf.hhs.gov/emergency/topic_childcare.cfm

http://www.fafsa.ed.gov/

http://studentaid.ed.gov/

http://www.whitehouse.gov/the-press-office/president-obama-announces-steps-reduce-dropout-rate-and-prepare-students-college-an

Singh S, Darroch JE. Adolescent pregnancy and childbearing: levels and trends in developed countries. Family Planning Perspectives 2000;32(1):14–23.

Hoffman SD. By the Numbers—The Public Costs of Teen Childbearing. Washington, DC: National Campaign to Prevent Teen Pregnancy; 2006.

Perper K, Peterson K, Manlove J. Diploma attainment among teen mothers. Child Trends, Fact Sheet Publication #2010-01: Washington, DC: Child Trends;2010.

Hoffman SD. Kids Having Kids: Economic Costs and Social Consequences of Teen Pregnancy. Washington, DC: The Urban Institute Press; 2008.

CPSIA information can be obtained
at www.ICGtesting.com
Printed in the USA
FSOW03n0646291215
15071FS